Temperance and
Cascade River State Parks

Porcupine Mountains

MN

Grand Island

Tenderfoot Reserve

ME

Hemlock Trail

Williams Woods

Nancy Brook

Ampersand Mountain

VT

NH

Vaughan Woods

MI

Cathedral Pines

Lisha Kill

Mohawk State Forest

WI

NY

Ice Glen

MA

Watkins Glen

CT

RI

Nerstrand Big Woods

Allegany State Park

Salt Springs

Bent of the River

IA

Minister Creek

Ricketts Glen

Stephens State Park

Cook Forest

McConnells Mill

Bull's Island

Goll Woods

PA

Alan Seeger

Gebhard Woods

Beaver Creek

NJ

Laurel Hill

OH

Ohiopyle

Patapsco
Valley

Swallow Falls

MD

DC

DE

Cathedral State Park

Rock Creek

Blackwater Falls

WV

Whiteoak Canyon

IL

IN

Montpelier

Red River Gorge

VA

MO

Hemmer Woods

KY

NC

Great Smoky Mountains

Savage Gulf

TN

Joyce Kilmer

Tallulah Gorge

Cloudland Canyon

Congaree

SC

AR

Sipsey Wilderness

Awendaw Passage

GA

MS

AL

Cumberland Island

LA

FL

AMERICA'S GREAT
FOREST TRAILS

TERRAIN ELEVATION

- 8,000 feet
- 6,000 feet
- 4,000 feet
- 2,000 feet
- 1,000 feet
- 500 feet

Highlands Hammock

PUERTO RICO

El Yunque

Miles

0   200

AMERICA'S GREAT

FOREST TRAILS

100 WOODLAND HIKES OF A LIFETIME

AMERICA'S GREAT
FOREST TRAILS
100 WOODLAND HIKES OF A LIFETIME

Text and Photographs by

TIM PALMER

RIZZOLI
NEW YORK

New York · Paris · London · Milan

CONTENTS

PART ONE

TREES, FORESTS, AND TRAILS

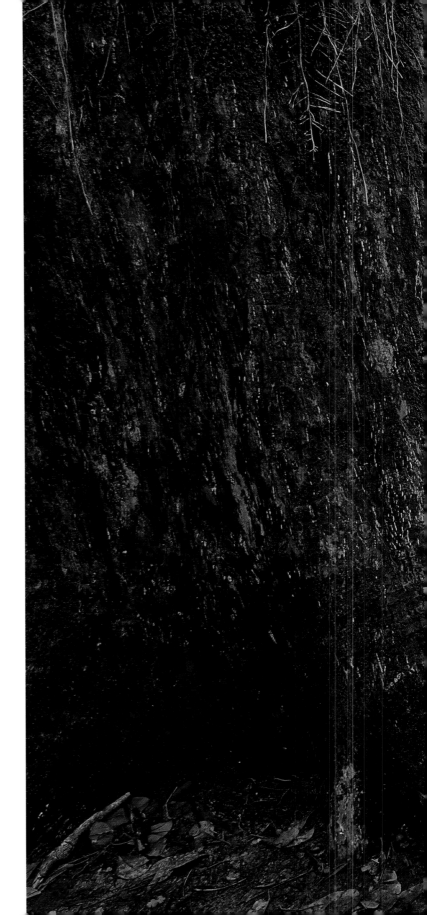

THE ALLURE OF THE FOREST

MANY OF US HAVE LIVED IN THE SHADE of maples, beeches, and sycamores across their territory from the Atlantic Ocean to the Great Plains. If not there, maybe you know the resinous scent of pines, firs, and spruces in the mountain terrain of the West, or the comfort of California's oaks that arc overhead like guardians of whole landscapes. Or perhaps you live among the towering conifers of the Pacific Northwest. As John Muir wrote in the year 1900, "Going to the woods is going home."

Forests cover a third of the country, and it tends to be the part where most people live. Even residents of western drylands know the elegance of cottonwoods along rivers and streams. We live with trees and we belong with trees, going back through whole generations, civilizations, and epochs of evolution. So it's no wonder that—beyond *living* in forests—we also like to *go* there for relaxation, comfort, and adventure, or simply to appreciate what many consider the ultimate in natural beauty.

People love to walk in the woods. Many of us feel attachment to our own native forest, but it's also interesting to see the life that thrives elsewhere and enjoy the mix of trees that makes each region of our country special— from tropical palms to alpine spruces, from brushy little sumacs so crimson in autumn to towering sequoias that humble everyone who gazes up from below. For many of us, taking a stroll beneath a living canopy of branches arcing overhead is the most reliable, affordable, and healthy way to feel good.

Forests are places to see and appreciate not only the dazzling diversity of trees—up to 40 species per acre in some parts of the Appalachian Mountains and 800 species nationwide—but also the intricate mosaic of shrubs and ground cover, or the splash of wildflowers where a ray of sun reaches the ground. A forest is a whole ecosystem, down to tiny building

PREVIOUS SPREAD: Tulip trees and other eastern hardwoods shade the trail at Patapsco Valley State Park in Maryland.

An ancient ausubo tree towers over Puerto Rico's El Yunque National Forest.

blocks in lichens, fungi, and bacteria. At the other end of the scale, redwoods are record holders for sheer mass of living matter, exceeding tropical rain forests in biomass per acre. Mature eastern forests are equally impressive in their way. All members of this arboreal community are important to the earth's life-support systems and thereby to every one of us.

Forest trails can take us to all of this, and also to adventure. Like others, I was thrilled by childhood explorations in the woods, and my adventures continue. With a sense of both discovery and appreciation, those experiences led me to create the book in your hands.

We can all go to the woods for unexpected rewards and fresh frontiers, no matter how near or far from home, no matter who else has been there before us, and no matter how many times we've padded down the same path, because that path is always different. You never know what will happen. On a woodland trail I recently encountered the first wolverine I've ever seen, this magical moment occurring after decades of watching for one of the elusive big relatives of the weasel. On another outing just months ago, an unexpected snowstorm dusted every branch and transformed the late-autumn landscape into a fantasy of white while I watched.

Perhaps more than anything, I value my woodland walks for the sense of total engagement they make possible. While I look to the trail ahead, listen to warblers in the canopy, and feel the organic texture of ground underfoot, the rest of the world disappears. With comforting familiarity near my home and the intrigue of destinations spanning the map of our country, forest trails lead me to an earth that's larger and more beautiful than anything I would otherwise know or imagine. When I return from these walks, I feel not only refreshed, but also motivated to live life fuller in both routine and uncharted ways.

Having grown up in Pennsylvania—literally Penn's Woods—and now living in Oregon—unequivocally a state of trees—my endorsement of woodland walks comes easily and honestly for me. But forests are the preferred landscape for many people, and in any one of the other states a hike among trees can be a universal contributor to happiness and peace of mind.

So let's go! For a day of exploration to the great unknown or for a retreat to a comforting glade or grove, choose a path close by or perhaps on your next vacation. On the pages that follow, I will share images and details of 100 woodland walks that have enriched my life and that I hope will enrich yours as well.

Chestnut oaks and associated hardwoods fill the Appalachian forest near Charlottesville, Virginia, where Steve Schmitz enjoys a morning walk.

TREES AND LIFE ON EARTH

WHAT ARE FORESTS FOR, ANYWAY? Why are they important? And what can a walk in the woods reveal?

Let's start with this: we inhale what trees exhale, and vice versa, and it's hard to imagine a more intimate relationship between living organisms than that. Through tiny pores called stomata, leaves absorb carbon dioxide from the atmosphere and then expel oxygen. Though most of the earth's oxygen comes from algae in the oceans, trees produce it as well, and forest organisms—including insects, birds, and we mammals—consume that oxygen and breathe out carbon dioxide, a perfect symbiotic match with the trees overhead.

Trees come the closest one might imagine to creating something out of nothing, which makes them particularly impressive. These are the world's largest, heaviest, tallest, most substantial organisms, and they are made essentially from air. After inhaling carbon dioxide from the atmosphere, trees convert it through photosynthesis to solid carbon in the form of limbs, trunks, and roots, amassing tons of wood and living tissue that can reach hundreds of feet into the sky. This phenomenon occurs in the woods every day, all day long, spring through fall. To witness one of the most fundamental acts of creation, just watch a tree.

The exchange of vital gasses between us and trees is just the starting point in our relationship. Many of us grow up with trees outside our windows and doors, and when we go for walks, we go to the woods, whether in a park nearby, on the Appalachian Trail with its 2,200 miles of forest, or in an oceanfront grove along the Pacific coast. If trees don't already exist, we plant them along our streets and in our yards, even if we have to rake the leaves five times in the fall. We also depend on what's made from trees and the larger and dependent forest environment, and the products include far

Redwoods and Pacific rhododendron catch early morning rays as the sun begins to break through overhead fog in California's Del Norte Coast Redwoods State Park.

intercepting atmospheric droplets and accumulating up to 30 inches a year in fog drip, which nourishes the entire forest with a perfectly suitable substitute for rain when in summertime real rain doesn't fall.

We're nourished directly by nuts, fruits, and seeds that trees produce, and so are myriad forms of life. The forest biome is the earth's richest and greatest in mass, its web of pulsing organic vitality extending from fungi and insects underfoot, through roots, ground covers, shrubs, saplings, and tree trunks, all the way to crowns made of limbs, leaves, and needles—the skyscrapers of the natural world. The forest zone houses thousands of creatures, microscopic to moose.

Trees fill the air space all around us, sometimes blocking the entire sky from view, yet half the biomass of many trees lies underground, where the roots absorb water and team up with mycorrhizal fungi. These are not just musty invisible parasites in the dirt but fibrous organisms that beneficially hug tree roots and help them in collecting water and taking up phosphorus, nutrients, and minerals. Firs, cedars, spruces, and all the choice trees for lumber depend on these fungi hitchhiking their livelihood on tiny root hairs, as they do with deciduous beeches, oaks, and walnuts. Fungi in humus bolster the growth rates of virtually all trees. The take-home lesson is this: for a forest to be productive, it requires healthy soil that is saturated with hidden microbial life and not damaged by earthmoving, compaction from heavy equipment, herbicides, scarring, or baking in the sun when shade overhead is removed.

Above ground—but still unnoticed much of the time—a hundred species of lichens live in the canopies of some northwestern forests. Essentially fungi wrapped around algae, lichens, along with mosses, can equal four times the weight of the leaves on some trees—even on the species called bigleaf maple, whose leaves are, well, *big*. Serving essential purposes, lichens and mosses become building blocks of immense forest ecosystems by trapping moisture that then drips down tree trunks to water the roots. Lichens fall to the ground when weighted by heavy snowfalls and serve as emergency forage for deer converging under the canopy.

Seen here in mixed shade and light at Nerstrand Big Woods State Park in Minnesota, sugar maple leaves are among the most effective foliage in absorbing energy of the sun for photosynthesis.

OPPOSITE: In the dampness of low-lying clouds, predawn light mystifies the woods at West Virginia's Spruce Knob and its medley of birches, ashes, maples, and oaks. Appalachian trees supplement rainfall by harvesting atmospheric moisture that condenses against branches and drips to the ground and the awaiting roots.

more than endless permutations of paper and lumber. For example, medicines derived from plants and microbes in forests account for 40 percent of all commercial drugs.

Trees and forests offer protection, not just in the shade they cast, but also from wind and storms that can rage outside a grove but scarcely ripple within. I feel this often at my home along the coast of Oregon, where storms each winter blast at hurricane force yet become muted and subdued by just a few Sitka spruces boldly guarding everything downwind—in this case, my porch and a whole continent to the east.

While blocking the wind, trees also intercept atmospheric moisture. Not counting the obvious rain and snowfall, the crowns of tall trees in the East can harvest five inches of precipitation yearly from cloud-laden, gaseous moisture that simply blows against the branches and foliage of trees, condenses there, and drips down to the roots. The great forests of the West Coast do even better with their larger "needle-sheds" of foliage and twigs

A variety of animals also hide as unnoticed players in endless episodes of forest drama. The canopy of a Douglas fir forest can contain 6,000 species of arthropods—insects, spiders, millipedes, and other faunal relatives. Salamanders—amphibians—account for more biomass per acre than any mammal in eastern deciduous forests; two dozen species might hide on the forest floor, processing nutrients of the 10 million leaves that can fall on a single acre annually. We see the secretive little amphibians less often than deer because they live so inconspicuously. But if they disappeared, a whole ecosystem would collapse. Other creatures likewise play critical roles in the maintenance of forests, which is a two-way street because all those creatures depend on the woods every day of their lives.

In healthy forests, warblers and dozens of other songbird species are difficult to see because they flitter in the tops of deciduous trees eating insects, which would overrun our own society if the forest-dwelling birds didn't keep bug numbers in check. Seeking family ties in springtime, those same birds sing their hearts out—a wild orchestra resonating widely, bursting with proud announcements of woodland life.

Lower down on those trees, dark cavities aren't just holes in rotten old trunks, but homes to chickadees, nuthatches, woodpeckers, owls, mergansers, raccoons, and others needing shelter. Underneath, deer that cannot kick or push snow out of the way find shelter beneath pines and hemlocks during the harshest winter storms. Some oak trees produce 28,000 acorns a year, a nutritious food source at the top of wildlife's menu—as gobbling wild turkeys attest while they scratch the duff for the nourishing nuts. They're not alone. The *Guide to Wildlife Food Habits* cites 96 species of animals that eat acorns, 97 counting *Homo sapiens*; the Gambel oak is my favorite for prepping to eat.

The workings of the forest are not only critical to the plants and animals that live there, but also to the health of a greater community. We know how important heating and cooling systems are to our homes. Well, it's the forests that help regulate the temperature of the big home—the earth—by cooling it with shade in summer and warming it with shelter in winter. In a mature hemlock grove, temperatures in July can be 15 degrees Fahrenheit cooler on the forest floor than at the sunlit treetops above, while in winter it's warmer on the ground than it would otherwise be owing to the dense overhead canopy that traps heat and conserves it through the night. Practical effects extend to suburban neighborhoods; air-conditioning

costs in sweltering Atlanta can be reduced by 40 percent if a homeowner plants just three trees.

Values of forests include such unexpected phenomena as the accumulation of fallen trees in streams. Aquatic health in many waterways depends on the unsung virtues of submerged trunks and the buildup of logjams that slow the current and trap gravel where fish can spawn. The logs deflect currents and create pools where fish feed and rear. Those streams support 5 to 50 times the number of salmon as logged watersheds having no large woody debris, according to biologists Chris Maser and James R. Sedell in *From the Forest to the Sea*.

Getting even more fundamental here, the forests are a backstage operative in the hydrologic cycle that's essential to all. Root masses and accumulated duff soak up rainfall and snowmelt, holding and then releasing them by way of springflows from groundwater later on, decreasing flood levels and providing natural storage that dwarfs, by far, all the dammed-up

OPPOSITE: Mosses and lichens beneficially attached to trunks and branches can total four times the weight of leaves on bigleaf maples such as this one in Oregon.

Though threatened with extinction across its range in the West, a red-legged frog finds a good home among undisturbed forests at Prairie Creek Redwoods State Park in California.

reservoirs ever built on rivers. According to biologists Reed F. Noss and Allen Y. Cooperrider in *Saving Nature's Legacy*, an undisturbed forest floor in the Northwest can absorb 12 inches of rainfall in an hour—a fact that would make floods far less frequent if the forest floors had not been badly disturbed. During summer, overhanging limbs shade creeks and rivers, keeping them cool and hospitable for aquatic life. It's the trees as much as the water that make trout fishing possible.

Runoff from healthy forests is clean, unlike the muddy flows from cutover land crisscrossed by roads or blanketed with farms. This is because organic matter falling from trees protects the forest floor. In an area near my home where soil has been scraped bare by recent logging, I've found that the shield created by a single alder leaf that had fallen before an autumn rainstorm possesses the remarkable ability to keep the soil beneath it intact while pelting rain washes away all the soil around

Leaves of an alder tree have fallen on terrain made bare by logging. After heavy rain, the leaves remain on pedestals of soil an inch high while the bare soil around them is washed away by raindrops to muddy the nearest stream. The pedestals illustrate the erosion protection that even a single leaf on the ground provides.

OPPOSITE: Hemlock roots at Lisha Kill Natural Area in New York lace the soil and armor its surface with a protective shield. This prevents erosion and literally holds the earth together.

the leaves to a depth of an inch. The guardian leaves remain like a cap on top of vertical pedestals of soil one inch high.

Buffers of forest alongside waterways also filter runoff seeping or streaming down from land up above by causing the stormwater to settle in the spongelike organic duff before the runoff reaches the stream. In this way, floodplain forests effectively serve as water-treatment systems for whole communities and vast landscapes, and they do it for free as long as the forests remain intact and protected.

Because most of the nation's drinking water is the runoff from forests, their protection is essential to public health. Facing costs of $8 billion for added treatment plants to make water drinkable, New York City opted to spend $1 billion in the 1990s to protect the forested watersheds surrounding the Hudson River reservoirs by acquiring development rights—an investment that paid off with continued water quality.

Forests literally hold the earth together. The masses of roots and humus not only build the soil from an inorganic smorgasbord of minerals into a spicy recipe for life, but also physically bind the soil in place. They stabilize the banks of streams, and the root masses woven through the ground prevent entire mountainsides from turning into Jell-O when wetted. Trees are the greatest guardian of property one could imagine.

Now we find that forests are even critical to the climate sustaining our entire world. Mainly composed of carbon, trees occupy the front line of defense against global warming. This problem is principally caused by the burning of earth's fossil fuel reserves—coal, oil, and natural gas—which converts solid or liquid carbon to gaseous carbon dioxide. Accumulating in the atmosphere, this gas warms the earth by allowing sunlight in but preventing the heat's escape; the atmospheric carbon acts like the roof of a greenhouse. This process created benefits when we needed the added heat to prep the cold rock of earth for the flourishing of life, but the effect is now perversely overdone. Since the Industrial Revolution in the early 19th century, carbon dioxide has increased by about 40 percent owing to our burning of fossil fuels, and the problem is growing rapidly with monumental disruptions to life.

For starters, the warming atmosphere heats the oceans. Warm water occupies more space than cold water, and when this principle of high school physics plays out on three-quarters of the globe's surface, the level of the seas rise, causing coastal erosion, flooding, and loss of land, along with whatever was built there. The warming climate also melts the polar ice caps, creating more ocean water and additional rise, which is increasing at an alarming rate as large portions of the ice caps melt. In 2014, the world's

top experts on the United Nations' Intergovernmental Panel on Climate Change predicted a sea level rise of up to six feet during this century, which would flood vast coastal areas, including many cities. More recent calculations in 2020 predicted a larger and more rapid rise, and official estimates of the severity of global warming have consistently been underestimated.

Warming will render entire agricultural and forest regions unusable owing to heat and associated changes in climate. Floods will increase as more precipitation arrives as rain and less as snow, and as storms intensify. The new climate will displace trees and other plant species from their home ranges faster than they can migrate toward the colder poles—the adjustment needed is 10 times faster than any known rate in the past. Forest fires have become more intense in a trend that will only worsen. Regrowth of forests will be handicapped by drier conditions. Warm-weather diseases, such as malaria and a host of viruses, will proliferate, along with severe hurricanes, which are caused by overheated ocean water. Because of the warming climate, the Rocky Mountain Climate Organization and Union of Concerned Scientists projected that by 2060 aspen trees across six states will be reduced by 60 percent; conifers may be eliminated by half.

Of course, we have to quit burning fossil fuels so these matters don't forever worsen, but it's already too late to avoid disruptive changes. In the face of atmospheric turmoil, it's forests that offer some hope. Trees do exactly the opposite of what we do when we burn fossil fuels. They take carbon out of the atmosphere and sequester it in their wood, where it's not only harmless but also beneficial. One tree can absorb 26 to 48 pounds of carbon a year; an acre of forest can absorb 10 tons. The key to this process is keeping old-growth and large trees alive; they are the ones that store the most carbon. Once logged, most of the carbon in trees rapidly escapes to the atmosphere through rot and burning of nondurable lumber and paper products. The new trees that replace the old ones might take a hundred years or more just to equal the sequestration value of the big trees on the day they were cut, let alone the amount those old trees would have grown in the intervening century. (Unlike we mammals and most other living creatures, trees continue to grow as long as they live.)

Furthermore, forests locally soften the effects of global warming by shading streams and landscapes, absorbing runoff from the intensified storms, and providing habitat to increasingly stressed wildlife. Unforeseen by most people just a few decades ago, the climate crisis has emerged as the central issue affecting the fate of the earth, and forests are critical to solutions on the path that must be followed if we're to sustain life as we know it, including our own. So it's with gratitude to trees that I take my walks in the woods.

All this praise of forests would not be complete without at least some mention of what we've done with our woods. To understand the modern landscape of America, it's important to know that nearly all the original forest has been cut down. While new forests are growing on much of that cutover acreage, the clearing for farms and land development has reduced the area of forest by a third since European settlement. The reduction lies mainly in the East and Midwest, where 280 million acres are now cultivated in crops, with the most acreage in pasture, hay, and corn for cattle, chickens, and pigs. Forests are also eliminated to make room for houses, roads, and other development. According to the Department of Agriculture in *Land Use Changes in Forestry in the United States*, about 500,000 acres nationwide continue to be converted to urban and agricultural use each year.

Among the great acreage that has been cut once or multiple times and now regrows, the conditions are vastly altered and the habitat for much of life reduced or eliminated. In the 48 contiguous states, only a few percent of the forest remains as old growth, meaning a forest that has been living for a long time without interruption by logging and that retains its rich diversity of life and robust ecological interactions. Even in the Pacific Northwest, known for its ancient forests, only 10 percent of the prelogging tapestry of woodland remains. That figure is zero for many regions of the country.

This all leads to a distressing statistic: distinguished biologist E. O. Wilson has estimated that ecosystems can generally tolerate up to a 90 percent reduction of their extent, but losses beyond that result in total collapse. Partial collapse occurs far sooner. Biologists Noss and Cooperrider have estimated that we must protect half the landscape to ensure health of natural ecosystems. All this points to the need to safeguard what remains of our old forests and to restore whatever is possible to earlier conditions. Nationwide, virtually all the old growth still standing can be found on public land. Wilderness designations or parks ban logging (and the resulting ecological transformation) on only about half of that tiny portion of America with uncut forest still remaining.

While forest issues are often portrayed as a choice between wood products and healthy forest ecosystems, scientists today recognize that

All trees absorb gaseous carbon dioxide from the atmosphere and convert it to solid carbon in their trunks, limbs, and roots.
At the Ross Creek Cedars Scenic Area in Montana, western redcedars sequester carbon in great amounts.

if we are to continue logging—and, for that matter, living—we need healthy forests from the soil on up. Trees are vital elements in a life-support system that's far greater than only themselves; they're not just sticks stuck in dirt, awaiting our next harvest.

Meanwhile, air pollution has destroyed forest health and attacked the ability of many trees to grow and resist disease. With the trees' immune systems crippled by foul air and heavy-handed logging, invasions of exotic plants, fungi, and insects now strike down one tree species after another. Eastern hemlocks, white ashes, American elms, valley oaks, white pines, sugar maples, flowering dogwoods, American beeches, and others are now plagued by exotic pests that weaken or kill the trees.

Biologists maintain that damage from air pollution makes the trees more susceptible to invasions by pathogens that could otherwise be resisted. Acid rain, for example, tarnishes waxy surfaces of leaves, leaving them vulnerable to unfriendly bacteria. Moreover, air polluted with aluminum, nickel, and lead dissolves in the soil, where tree roots take up those toxic elements.

Yet another reason for forest collapse has been our misguided compulsion to suppress every natural forest fire. Before white settlement, fires caused by lightning often walked through the woods, burning fallen limbs and brush, keeping the understory open and parklike, and encouraging the growth of large trees, grasses, and wildlife forage. The crowns of tall trees, such as ponderosa pines, were out of reach from flames because frequent small blazes pruned back the fuel at the bases of the trees, whose bark was thick and fire-resistant. After cutting those large trees, crowded seedlings germinated and multiple saplings competed for space. Now, without the large, old, fire-resistant trees, and without the thinning action of frequent low-level flames, a tangle of unhealthy forests has taken over— monocultures prone to disease and superheated flames that burn like gasoline once ignited, which in the long term is inevitable with both lightning strikes and human-caused wildfires. With global warming's higher temperatures, lower humidity, and intensified hot winds, the stage is set for catastrophe, and, in fact, cataclysmic fires have become a plague, torching not only the woods but entire urban communities as well.

Our stewardship of forests, and the trees' abilities to withstand the stresses on their lives, are what define the term "forest health"—not only a

Old trees grow thick bark and drop their lower limbs, becoming fire-resistant, with resulting low-level burns like this one among ponderosa pines south of Bend, Oregon. The older trees survive the onslaught of fire, grow larger, and become even more fire-resistant with age.

prerequisite for production of lumber, but also a condition that resists fire, supports a full complement of native plant and animal species, and offers productive habitat to nurture them. Forest health means having plant life that builds soil and protects it from erosion; that moderates floods, droughts, and the weather; and that provides for people's needs without a loss of ability to provide for those needs in the future—in short, the kind of conditions that predated heavy-handed encroachment on the forest environment.

Amid discouraging losses, there is still cause for hope. In the unlikely woods of West Virginia, trees had been stripped from virtually all the state but regrew to cover 87 percent. Much will be cut again, but hopefully without the careless abandon of the past.

Most important, people increasingly recognize that the forest's larger life-support system requires attention. Air pollution and global warming need to be reduced if our forests are to survive as sources of life and regulators of vital hydrologic, climatic, and ecological processes. While the loss of our original forests has been almost comprehensive, and the pressures and problems affecting our woodlands remain extreme, we've also had a remarkable movement to save ancient groves, to protect forests, and to restore some of what has been lost.

Pressed by the American Forestry Association (now American Forests), Congress in 1891 passed the Forest Reserve Act, leading to the creation of the Forest Service in 1905 and establishment of the national forest system, which now includes 193 million acres as public land managed by the federal government, mostly in the West but with important tracts in the East as well. Within these federal forests, 158,000 miles of trails wind through the woodlands. The trees in this public estate absorb 10 percent of the global-warming carbon emissions of the United States each year. However, national forest status does not automatically mean that forests will be protected. In fact, industrial timber interests dominated the agency for years. But, from the 1980s onward, laws have required that at least some ecological concerns be addressed.

To protect selected federal land from logging and development, Congress passed the Wilderness Act in 1964. Safeguarded wilderness areas have grown to be 20 percent of the national forest system, though that is still only 2.7 percent of the United States outside Alaska. For years, much of this set-aside acreage was at high and lightly forested elevations, but since the 1970s increasing attention has focused on woodlands as well. In 1978, Oregon's French Pete Creek was one of the first wilderness areas set aside even though it included commercial timber.

With recognition that intrinsic forest values deserve protection outside the relatively small wilderness system, laws such as the National Forest Management Act of 1976 were passed, and administrative rules were adopted to protect forest values including endangered species, riparian or riverfront habitat, and roadless areas that remain wild. Virtually all these measures are under current attack by interests that would like to open up federal land now managed for natural qualities.

Starting in the late 1800s but picking up momentum from 1980 onward, efforts to protect forests stemmed, in part, from the importance of natural woodlands as described in hiking guides and natural history literature. *America's Great Forest Trails* was prepared in that tradition of recognizing the value of our unspoiled or recovering forests and of guiding people toward better knowledge and appreciation of them.

While the trails in this book were not selected solely for their protected status, many of them lie in areas set aside from clear-cutting, roadbuilding, and land development. These include national parks, wilderness areas, and state parks.

Given the deep connections between people, trees, and forests, it's no wonder that many of us appreciate a walk in the woods. The attraction is integral to our psyches, spirits, and bodies. The piney or leafy aroma of the woods invigorates our senses when we enter the groves and glades. Short strolls in the woods can hit the spot for quick exposure to the natural world. Longer walks allow the joys and pleasures to accumulate and can infuse us with the wealth of natural wonders found no other way.

So come along on the woodland walks I've been privileged to photograph and write about. The allure of the forest might be just outside the door, or at the edge of town, or in a park within a short drive. Spice up your life with a visit, and join the greater community of nature through your own walk in the woods.

As intense heat and wind become more common in the age of global warming, and with thickets of young forests replacing the older fire-resistant trees that have been logged out, blazes intensify, like this inferno near the border of Yellowstone National Park in 1988.

TRAILS TO WOODLAND WONDERS

THIS BOOK DESCRIBES 100 FOREST hikes and woodland walks across America. Any number of other destinations could have been chosen, and readers will have their own favorites. So why these 100?

I must admit to being fond of big trees and impressed with their gravitas and symbolism of life, so many of the hikes here lead to impressive large trees. But this is not a compendium of those, nor a wish list of the tallest. Also, while I value the chance to see all the different kinds of trees in America, the paths outlined here were not selected for the purpose of seeing every species. Rather, I looked broadly to forests that are beautiful and to trails that are rewarding for any number of reasons, including their pristine nature or escape to places I'm tempted to call perfect. Some locations were chosen because they show possibilities for restoration—for what forests are becoming, once again, after an era of loss. Not all regions are equal, but I sought memorable hikes in all the forest types nationwide. I looked for woods that were close to cities and for a few others as far away as I could go. I've personally walked on all the paths described here, though for a few I've not yet covered the full distance.

This is not so much a "bucket list." Rather, my intent here is to stir readers' interest in walking the woods wherever you are. Missing in this book are hundreds of excellent hikes that will be closer to home and more convenient for you. So go there! Most of us don't have to burn a lot of gasoline or jet fuel to visit a great forest.

Along this line, in the age of the climate crisis, my enticement to hike is not meant to encourage more driving and burning of fossil fuels, but rather less of it, with enjoyment of free time *outside* the car—on foot instead of on wheels. And even if you have to drive for a forest vacation, it's better to drive and then hike than it is to drive and then drive some more.

Members of the local Kalmiopsis Audubon Society join for a weekend walk on Humbug Mountain in the coastal forest of southern Oregon.

I also regard trails here in our country as a sensible alternative to traveling farther. No one needs to go halfway around the globe to find a memorable woodland walk. According to Manfred Lenzen in *Nature Climate Change*, eight percent of greenhouse gas emissions owe to tourism, with international air travel accounting for much of it. Here in the United States many of us are fortunate to have splendid forests where we can walk near home, or we can minimize our burning of fossil fuel by lingering with extended hikes or by clustering our outings—for example, in the redwoods of California or the White Mountains of New Hampshire. Walk more; drive less!

The selection of trails in this book includes both short strolls and epic backpack expeditions, though most of these outings can be done without special skills, equipment, or endurance. Many of the trails are very short—sometimes distressingly so owing to centuries of logging and development that have reduced the finest woodlands to small tracts. Short trails, however, can sometimes be linked to longer hikes.

I strived to include America's classic woodlands, from hemlocks in New England to astonishing oaks on Georgia's Cumberland Island. Our oldest trees are bristlecone pines of the interior West. The largest grow in Sequoia National Park, the tallest in Northern California. All are included here, as are modest birches and aspens that pioneer after fires, and head-high vine maples that brighten forest scenes with starry leaves catching sunlight and seeming to magnify it at eye level.

While all seasons have their appeal, my favorite times are May, when leaves burst forth in patterns of pale green, and autumn, when air is crisp and fall colors peak with a special show in all regions, but an extravagant one in New England, the northern Midwest, and the Appalachians. Summer is fine, and carefree in its way, but the bugs can be annoying. The heat in summer can be prohibitive in the Southwest and South, and increasingly stifling elsewhere, except for the highcountry of the West and along the Pacific coast. Low-elevation and low-latitude locations, including the South and Southwest, are prime in winter, and in colder climes cross-country skiing reveals its own woodland beauty for adventurers who are savvy in snow.

Let's recognize that any outdoor adventure can involve hazards. Information here is offered as accurately as possible, but be aware that conditions change and parameters of safe travel vary with the individual, season, and weather. All hikers must assume responsibility for their own safety and make accurate assessments of hazards. That's part of the fun and adventure! That also makes outdoor explorations more exciting and interesting than strolling on the sidewalk or, for that matter, sitting on the couch, where spending too much time is likely to be more dangerous than hiking even in difficult terrain.

Hikers need to know their own limitations, the conditions of the trail, and the weather forecast at the time of their outing. Because readers represent a wide range of abilities, information here is not a recommendation for any particular person to set off on any of these trails. In other words, guidance here is no substitute for common sense, prudence, experience, fitness, training, skill, safe weather, and competent personal assessment of dangers. Be equipped. Good footgear, warm garb, rain protection, and a water bottle are essential.

All that said, many of the hikes here fall under the easy category, and many are short outings to groves visited by people of all abilities. Hikers will still want to be alert to common hazards such as poison ivy and poison oak. Beware of rattlesnakes, copperheads, and cottonmouth moccasins when in their habitat, though they are rarely encountered on the trails described here. My defense is to watch where I step and stay on the path—where I can see the ground—when I'm in reptile-land.

Forest hikes can be buggy, especially early in summer, with mosquitoes and blackflies in the North, mosquitoes and no-see-ums in the South, and ticks throughout in wet seasons and thickets of grass. With tick-borne lime disease and mosquito vectors on the rise, concerns today have eclipsed those of the past when many of us dismissed bugs as a casual nuisance, even when they thickened the atmosphere. I now wear full-length clothing and pale colors, which attract mosquitoes less. Preferring natural repellants such as citronella, I find them effective for most bugs if reapplied often. DEET is a sure bet when the going gets tough. I apply it to my pant cuffs in tick country, but staying on trails when in grassy areas remains my first defense.

My directions to these trails assume that readers have a state road map. Brochures with details are often posted at trailheads within state parks or federal land. For longer hikes, or where linked paths make ambitious expeditions possible, many hikers will want a detailed map, available at outdoor stores, online, or through the National Park Service, Forest Service, Bureau of Land Management, or state park departments.

The path on Mount Theodore Roosevelt in South Dakota's Black Hills National Forest rises above a ponderosa pine forest and passes through an aspen grove at the summit.

Disorientation can occasionally take you somewhere you don't want to go. If a map and compass are not your primary means of navigation—as they are for me—they're important backups, especially for extended hikes.

While national and state parks have long charged entrance fees, some national forests now do this as a parking sticker. People who are over the age of 62 are eligible for a Lifetime Senior Pass good for federal sites. Apart from entrance fees at parks, most of the hikes in this book can be done without a permit. But for some overnight trips, especially in national parks, permits are needed, and some are tightly rationed. I note many of these in the following pages. If in doubt, check with the managing agency and apply for your permit ahead of time.

Permits are required for the simple reason that so many people want to see the most beautiful places. Some of the hikes in this book fall into that category. If you want to avoid crowds, favor weekdays and shoulder seasons, even pushing the envelope in early spring and late fall. During prime season, hitting the trail early or late in the day misses the rush, with the added benefit of beautiful low sunlight.

Remember, the upside to all those hikers seeing those forests is explained in this timeless axiom: We only care for the places we love, we only love the places we know, and we only know the places we see. Along this line, be attuned to your own effects on fragile landscapes. Never shortcut between switchbacks, which aggravates erosion. Avoid tramping through sensitive wetlands and on the desert's lichen-filled cryptogamic crust, identified by its textured dark color. If off-trail hiking there, step rock to rock or follow water-worn washes.

Before your outing, check your shoes for weed seeds hitchhiking from your previous trip. In heavily used areas, pack out toilet paper in a plastic bag—not as gross as it sounds. Minimize the scars of campfires, or don't build them; use a camp stove or, better, get creative with cold food, even overnight. It's just a meal. Respect others and wildlife by being quiet. Avoid harassing animals by approaching so close that they move away or change their behavior, even if it means missing the photo. Remember, while we might simply seek a good picture, a crucial dinner might be at stake for the animal or, worse, a pivotal compromise for the safety of it and its young. Quite honestly, my own wildlife pictures come not from stealthy efforts as a wildlife photographer pressing my prey, but from places such as national parks, where animals have become accustomed to people.

On a larger scale, care and stewardship of forests are critical not only for our outings, but also for the water we drink, wildlife we value, and essential workings of whole ecosystems that sustain life on earth. I encourage anyone who enjoys the wild forests of America to enlist in efforts to protect them. Think of it as the cost of admission. Join national groups such as the Wilderness Society, regional groups such as the Appalachian Mountain Club or Sierra Nevada Alliance, and also local land trusts, friends-of-forest organizations, and hiking clubs. Some groups—such as the Pacific Crest Trail Association, Appalachian Trail Club, and Siskiyou Mountain Club—maintain trails, which can be a lot of fun with some of the nicest people you're ever likely to meet.

Loving trees, learning about the importance of wild forests, and benefiting from exercise, fresh air, and the solace that comes with woodland walks are all reasons to visit the places in this book and beyond. Another reason is that these beloved strongholds of nature are changing. That's the way of the world, but many of the changes today are regrettable in the face of commodification, development, exotic pests, encroaching disease, and, most of all, the climate crisis. So enjoy the trails featured here, see your local forest while you can, and be inspired to follow a longer path to ensure that the best of nature endures for the next generation as well. Woodland adventures of many kinds await.

Winter storms pile snow on the limbs of red firs at Basin Peak near Donner Pass in California's Sierra Nevada.

FOLLOWING SPREAD: Sitka spruces and grand firs guard headlands above the Pacific Ocean at Oregon's Port Orford Heads State Park.

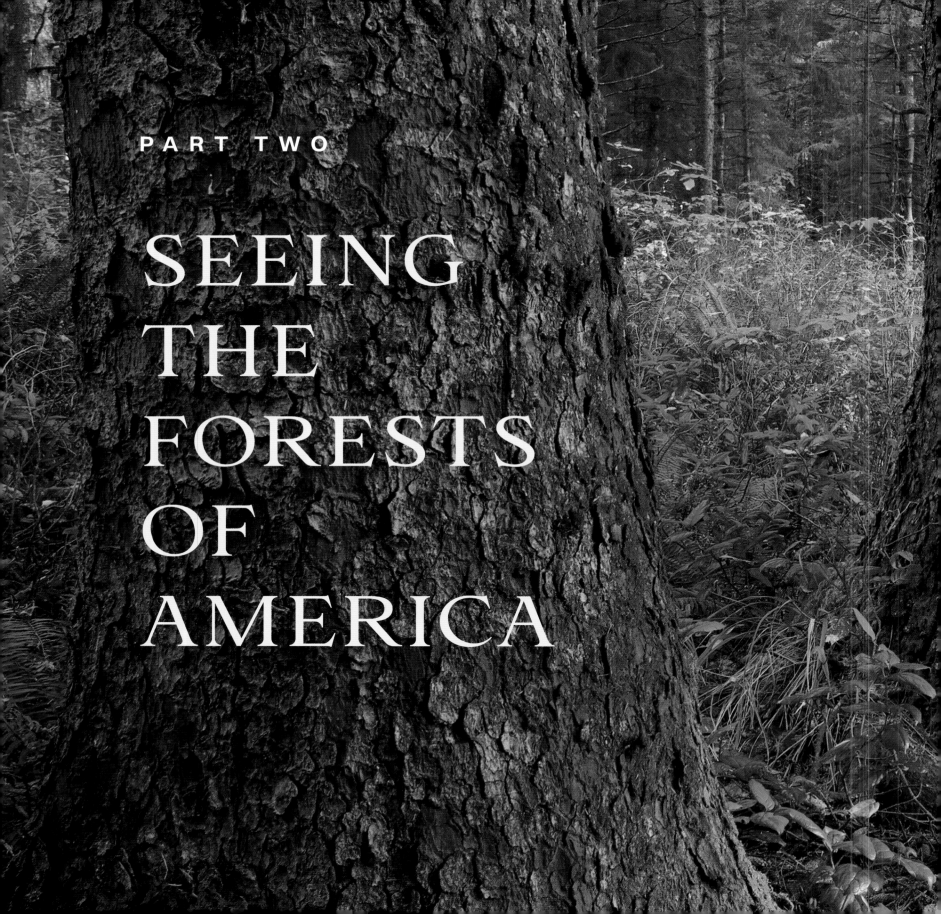

PART TWO

SEEING THE FORESTS OF AMERICA

NEW ENGLAND

Forests blanket New England—the quintessential territory of wooded mountains with villages and farms tucked into valleys and tree-lined byways and trails throughout. New England consists of Maine through Connecticut, and New York is included in this chapter for its similarities of glacier-shaped topography and sylvan cast of characters.

Woodlands here reflect the dominance of cold winters and the legacy of the Pleistocene's creeping wall of mile-thick ice reshaping everything in its path 15,000 years ago. As the last glacier receded, trees migrated back north from ice-free latitudes to claim their new frontier on glacial outwash. Cold-adapted species linger, with northern New England's somber tones of spruce, balsam fir, and hemlock that straddle the Canadian border.

Additional species fingered northward as the climate moderated and accommodated the mixed company of deciduous trees. Northern hardwoods now thrive with beeches, sugar maples, and red maples—foliage that blazes in color through October. Warmer weather in southern New England supports oaks, basswoods, sycamores, and ashes in a rich arboreal palate typical of forests farther south.

By the mid-1800s European settlers had cleared 80 percent of New England for agriculture. Seeking more amenable growing conditions, most farmers moved on. New woodlands sprang to life, and they now cover 80 percent of the land again after a remarkable experience in forest demise and recovery, which continues.

All but half of one percent of eastern forests were cut. In New England, only about 100 old-growth groves remain, and two-thirds of them total fewer than 100 acres each. The Adirondack Mountains of New York, where 69 percent of the region's unlogged forest can be found, are the primary exception to these statistics.

Favorites of many hikers are hemlocks with dark-green lacy foliage and trunks like cathedral columns when allowed to grow old. Unfortunately, the hemlocks have been attacked by an exotic insect, the woolly adelgid, which has spread from Virginia, where it was introduced with ornamental nursery stock imported from Japan in 1951. Adelgids now infest more than half the eastern hemlock's 23-state inventory, killing nearly all these stately conifers south of New York except for trees treated with insecticide in hopes that durable solutions will come with the introduction of biological predators—beetles carefully imported from Asia and the Pacific Northwest. New England states have fared better than those to the south; northern cold snaps tend to knock adelgids back, though not eliminate them. Surviving hemlocks are veritable redwoods of the East, with their height, their seniority dating back as many as 600 years where they haven't been logged, and their undeniable charisma within the forests around them.

Yankees love their woodland trails. More than in any other region, local land trusts have safeguarded tracts at the edges of towns where pathways beckon to all. One stellar national park—Acadia—and two national forests—White Mountain and Green Mountain—include hundreds of woodland walks. Many state parks have outstanding though mostly short paths. The Appalachian Trail links the entire region north to south, and to its west the Long Trail tracks the crest of Vermont's Green Mountains. Trail networks lace the Adirondack Park of New York, luring hikers since the first days of American tourism.

New England has the most distinctive contrast of seasonal forest transformation in the country. Spring, summer, fall, and winter make outings to the same woods vividly different each time. Winter is starkly elegant, with leafless branches articulated as if by a sharpened pencil in the hand of a skilled artist, all unified when the ground is blanketed by snow, which can linger for months. Long winters make the bursting buds of May welcome when the cold softens into damp, sweet-smelling iterations of springtime. Summer entices with its expected comforts, such as swimming holes enveloped in green foliage. Fall is unconditionally glorious with crisp days, cold nights, and colors that dazzle more than anywhere else in America.

Hemlock Trail, Acadia National Park

MAINE

LOCATION
south of Bar Harbor

LENGTH
2 miles out and back

DIFFICULTY
easy

TREE SPECIES
hemlocks, sugar maples,
red maples, beeches,
paper birches

HIGHLIGHTS
large hemlocks, northern
hardwoods

PREVIOUS SPREAD: The White Mountains
of northern New Hampshire preside as
one of the East's great forest regions. Here
sunrise breaks behind a ridge of white
pines. The foreboding red sky at morning
warns of an autumn storm's approach.

The trails of Acadia National Park feature
a forest recovering from not only the
last ice age, but also fires that have
burned across much of the park's
acreage. Here hemlocks, beeches, and
birches grow again in the rocky terrain.

OPPOSITE: At Acadia National Park,
Ann Vileisis, the author's wife, strolls
the Hemlock Trail through northern
hardwoods with mature hemlock
trees towering skyward.

This easy, popular trail introduces us to the forests of New England, showcasing mature eastern hemlocks and elegant members of the northern hardwoods community. Few tours of American forests can start farther north and east than this one; the trail begins 70 miles from Canada and 1 mile from the ocean, and it links with other paths that lead to overlooks within a stone's throw of Atlantic surf.

Eastern hemlocks are the big draw. Mature trees survived a 1947 fire on the east side of Acadia National Park's Mount Desert Island and now tower overhead. With cold winters, the hemlocks here have thus far been spared fatal infection by the invasive woolly adelgid. Park scientists monitor the grove for the unwelcome arrival of that exotic insect.

Virtually at sea level, with the ocean's tempering effect on climate, this trail is open year-round, with fog common in summer, fewer bugs by August, and then the joys of autumn.

From Bar Harbor, drive south and take the Park Loop Road east to the Sieur de Monts parking area at Wild Gardens of Acadia. Walk north from the visitor center on Jesup Path to the Hemlock Trail.

Paths link back to downtown Bar Harbor and the park's additional 120-mile trail network. Choices nearby include the oceanfront at Great Head to the south, plus a rewarding route to glaciated domes called The Bubbles. The entire park showcases northern trees reclaiming terrain once scraped bare by glaciers and partially burned later by wildfires.

Vaughan Woods
State Park

MAINE

LOCATION
northwest of Kittery

LENGTH
3 miles out and back

DIFFICULTY
easy

TREE SPECIES
eastern hemlocks, northern hardwoods

HIGHLIGHTS
dense hemlock groves

Hundred-year-old hemlocks rise over the forest floor and above tranquil waters of the Salmon Falls River at the border of New Hampshire, where deep shade and overbrowsing by deer have created an open understory in this 250-acre park. Hemlocks here are exposed to the sap-sucking woolly adelgid, but are treated with insecticide by park managers who are hopeful that biological controls will become effective. Best seen in late summer and fall, the park is closed in winter.

From I-95 at Kittery, take Route 236 north. Before South Berwick, turn left on Vine Street, jog right on Vaughans Lane, and then turn left on Oldfields Road.

A dense grove of hemlocks casts deep shade at Vaughan Woods State Park, and the conifers' fallen needles resist rot, all yielding a clear understory compared to other forests in the East. Lacking natural predators, an overpopulation of deer also consumes shrubbery and ground cover here and across many forests of the Northeast.

Nancy Brook Trail, White Mountain National Forest

LOCATION
north of Conway

LENGTH
1 to 6 miles out and back

DIFFICULTY
medium to strenuous

TREE SPECIES
white pines, red spruces, yellow birches, beeches

HIGHLIGHTS
recovering New England forest, cascading woodland stream

Like the rest of the East, the old growth of New Hampshire was nearly all cut, but 2,000 acres remain in scattered parcels of White Mountain National Forest and recovering second growth is a fine sample of what gives New England its wooded charm.

For a scenic path, visit Nancy Brook's northern hardwoods and red spruces. Many were dying at the height of acid-rain pollution in the 1980s, but since the Clean Air Act of 1990 acid has abated and the spruces have begun to recover.

From North Conway, drive northwest on Highway 302 past Bartlett, go 5 miles, and watch for Nancy Brook Trailhead on the left. Hike west through second growth and then into old yellow birches and red spruces, up to 6 miles out and back.

White Mountain National Forest offers 1,200 miles of hiking, including backpacking routes on the Appalachian Trail through weather-stunted forests of the Presidential Range and its six peaks bulging above timberline. With autumn foliage, bubbling streams, soaring summits rising from sheltered coves to timberline, and fewer bugs than the lake-studded outback of Maine or the Adirondack Mountains in New York, this is my favorite region for woodland hiking in New England.

Young beech trees with springtime's unfurling leaves magnify early morning sunlight on the Nancy Brook Trail in White Mountain National Forest.

OPPOSITE: Not far from Nancy Brook, and west of Conway, the Swift River invites streamfront strolling with cascading waters beneath elegant white pines and hardwoods. Loggers had cut virtually all the white pines, which had been the mainstay of northern forests from Maine through Wisconsin. Today the conifers are returning in robust numbers at sunlit openings and woodland edges across their wide range.

Williams Woods
Natural Area

LOCATION
south of Burlington, north
of Vergennes

LENGTH
0.5 miles

DIFFICULTY
easy

TREE SPECIES
sugar maples, bur oaks,
hemlocks

HIGHLIGHTS
old-growth hemlocks, oaks,
other hardwoods

Though only 25 acres, this forest showcases aged trees of a dozen species. Old groves of Williams Woods' caliber are surprisingly unusual for the tree-carpeted state of Vermont—literally named "green mountain" by Samuel de Champlain.

Though not especially fat or tall, hemlocks here date back three centuries. Rare outside the Midwest, bur oaks here are dated at 300 years according to old-growth aficionados Bruce Kershner and Robert T. Leverett in *The Sierra Club Guide to the Ancient Forests of the Northeast*.

To find this low-key grove bought by The Nature Conservancy in 1983, drive north from Vergennes on Highway 7 for 5 miles, go left on Stage Road, and drive 1 mile. At Greenbush Road, turn right, go 1.2 miles to the end of a field on the left, and watch for a small sign. Park along the road.

Though small, Williams Woods remains one of the finer old-growth forests in Vermont. Hemlocks, beeches, white oaks, sugar maples, and others catch low-angle rays of autumn's late-afternoon sunlight.

Mohawk Trail State Forest

MASSACHUSETTS

LOCATION
west of Greenfield

LENGTH
1 to 8 miles out and back

DIFFICULTY
medium

TREE SPECIES
white pines, northern red oaks, beeches, sugar maples, white ashes, hemlocks, bigtooth aspens, striped maples

HIGHLIGHTS
New England's overall tallest old-growth forest

Mohawk Trail State Forest is New England's tallest woodland. Here a northern red oak rises on the left and young beech trees fill the scene with yellow and amber leaves. Two older beeches, with smooth gray trunks, appear to resist beech bark disease, which otherwise ravages these magnificent trees once they grow beyond sapling size.

FOLLOWING SPREAD: Morning light has not yet reached the trunks of white pines and mixed hardwoods along the Deerfield River in Mohawk Trail State Forest.

Mohawk Trail and neighboring Savoy Mountain State Forests total 17,500 acres, including 700 acres of old growth with the second-largest expanse of tall trees in the Northeast, exceeded only by Pennsylvania's Cook Forest, according to tall-tree analyst Robert Leverett. Thirty-one white pines top 150 feet, and white ashes—still surviving the emerald ash borer as of 2020—reach 140 feet. Fifteen tree species are state champions for height.

The main path—a local segment of the Mahican-Mohawk Trail whose 100-mile route is still in progress—offers a big-tree tour above the Deerfield River, which is one of Massachusetts's finest scenic waterways. Hike to the Elder Grove of pines at the upstream, northwestern end of the state property. Big pines cluster in several other groves along the park road near the campground, group camping site, and slopes of Todd Mountain.

Following a map from the entrance station, take the Cold River Trail, turn left on the Mahican-Mohawk Trail, and go downriver.

From I-91 at Greenfield, turn west on Route 2, drive 22 miles, and then turn right into Mohawk Trail State Forest.

Ice Glen

MASSACHUSETTS

LOCATION
Stockbridge

LENGTH
1 to 3 miles out and back

DIFFICULTY
moderate

TREE SPECIES
white pines, hemlocks, sugar maples, beeches, gray birches, sweet birches, white ashes, northern red oaks

HIGHLIGHTS
tall white pines, hemlocks

At charming historic Stockbridge, this shaded rocky ravine is an easily reached pocket of rare ancient forest. The 25-acre tract, which seems like more, is managed by the Laurel Hill Association. It is credited with a 300-year-old white pine as the second-tallest tree in New England at 153 feet and the tallest hemlock at 137 feet.

From the parking lot, cross a Housatonic River footbridge to rocky terrain, presumably too rugged for harvesting in the region's logging heyday. To spare native plant life, avoid off-trail scrambling, tempting as it is. The chilled ravine is prime for hemlocks.

Late spring and fall are outstanding. In winter, be ready for—no surprise—ice, with its own beauty of rococo glazes refrozen nightly.

Take Highway 7 to midtown Stockbridge, turn east on Park Street, and drive to the end.

In the mixed forest of Ice Glen, morning sun breaks through where a northern red oak on the left rises among eastern hemlocks.

FOLLOWING SPREAD: The limb-filled crown of a white pine at Ice Glen branches out to catch light at the top of the ancient forest canopy (left). Ice Glen is known for its towering white pines, rising here above the last green leaves of a sugar maple in autumn (right).

Bent of the River Audubon Center

LOCATION
South Britain, west of Southbury

LENGTH
2 miles

DIFFICULTY
easy

TREE SPECIES
sycamores, sugar maples, hemlocks, beeches, dogwoods, white oaks

HIGHLIGHTS
large sycamores, Pomperaug River frontage

A flowering dogwood at Bent of the River Audubon Center bursts with full blooms in May. Many wild dogwoods have been infected by an invasive fungus, anthracnose, which cripples and kills the trees. Once common throughout their 29-state range, these beautiful trees have become rarer in recent decades.

OPPOSITE: Like other New England forests owned by local land trusts and conservation groups, Bent of the River invites visitors to walk its trails through the shade of hemlocks.

Bent of the River's mix of northern hardwoods, open fields, recovering forest, and riparian old growth offers an enchanting loop trail owned by Audubon Connecticut, which is open to the public for free. The 700 acres of hardwoods and hemlocks have recovered with classic New England charm at a historic farmstead along the banks of the Pomperaug River.

Accessible year-round, this preserve is striking in May when dogwoods bloom (provided the invasive anthracnose fungus doesn't get them), in autumn when New England's colors flare, and in winter when snow whitens the scene. And there's nothing wrong with summer either.

From I-84 exit 14 west of Southbury, drive north on Route 172 a mile to South Britain. Beyond the store, turn left, pass a monumental sycamore, go left into the preserve, and park on the right.

Take the trail along the Pomperaug, and don't miss a side path on the left into a floodplain sycamore grove. Farther on the main trail, mature sugar maples, beeches, oaks, and birches are followed by a loop through a dense hemlock and beech forest.

Ampersand Mountain, Adirondack Park

NEW YORK

LOCATION
west of Saranac Lake

LENGTH
1 to 6 miles out and back

DIFFICULTY
easy to strenuous

TREE SPECIES
yellow birches, sugar maples, hemlocks, red spruces, balsam firs, beeches, white pines

HIGHLIGHTS
old forest with wooded wetlands, mountain climb and view

Lower slopes of Ampersand Mountain shelter some of the oldest trees in the vast expanse of the Adirondack Park, including red spruce, balsam fir, eastern hemlock, and white pine. Hemlocks, birches, and beeches dominate the wooded wetland here with both the ancient and the young.

The 6-million-acre Adirondack Park is the largest "park" in the United States outside Alaska (Death Valley National Park is 3.4 million acres; Yellowstone is 2.2 million acres). An unusual mix, 2.6 million acres are owned by the state as the nation's only preserve constitutionally safeguarded as "forever wild," with commercial logging, dams, and most development banned. The other 3.4 million acres within the park's boundaries are private, including 105 villages and towns where reasonable state land-use restrictions apply. This is also one of America's oldest large parks, designated in 1892.

Unique in the United States, with lakes, glaciated peaks, and forested wildness, the Adirondacks' 100-mile-wide dome of rugged topography is related more to the Canadian Shield of Precambrian bedrock in Quebec and Ontario than to the Appalachians, which geologically lie to the east. Owing to harsh winters, spare glacier-scraped soils, and wetlands, tree sizes here are not large compared to the giants of the Smoky Mountains in the southern Appalachians, but the Adirondack Park has more acres of virgin old growth than any other eastern forest.

For a large stand of mixed conifers and hardwoods, Ampersand Mountain is hard to beat. Sugar maples and yellow birches join an unusual conifer quartet: eastern hemlocks, white pines, red spruces, and balsam firs are scattered through 2,000 old-growth acres. Most of the large trees appear at the beginning of the trail.

Autumn is fabulous in the Adirondacks; summer is beautiful but buggy. Winter is severe by any standard, when hiking with snowshoes becomes expeditionary.

From the town of Saranac Lake, take Route 3 southwest 8 miles to the Ampersand parking lot on the right and trailhead on the left. After 1.5 miles, a steep 1,900-foot climb graduates through multiple forest zones ramping to summit outcrops and views to Middle Saranac Lake's glassy lens and farther across a stormy sea of Adirondack peaks.

Ampersand is just one hike among the park's 2,000 miles of wooded trails featuring lakes, rivers, and rocky summits. Another favorite of mine is the trek up Owls Head Mountain (there are two; this one's off Route 73 west of Keene) to sky-high bedrock where jack pines brave the top and postcard views to Porter Mountain flame with October foliage.

The enthralling view from the summit of Owls Head Mountain opens a window to the Adirondack landscape and its brilliant October show of red maples, birches, and other hardwoods in yellow and orange. Jack pines cling to ancient rocks while an autumn storm chills the background.

Lisha Kill Natural Area

NEW YORK

LOCATION
northeast of Schenectady

LENGTH
1.5 miles

DIFFICULTY
easy

TREE SPECIES
hemlocks, white pines, northern red oaks, beeches

HIGHLIGHTS
old-growth eastern forest

This 108-acre preserve with old-growth conifers and hardwoods is a deeply shaded grove with trails looping throughout. Bought by The Nature Conservancy in 1964, the stand of hemlocks appeals in spring, summer, and fall; it is closed February through May.

Tucked away in unexpected suburbia, the preserve lies off the northeast corner of Schenectady. From I-87 at Latham, take exit 6, go left on Route 7 for 4.5 miles, and then turn right on Mohawk Road. At a T, go left on Rosendale Road, continue 1 mile while passing Lock 7 Road and River Road, and in 0.2 more miles park at an unlikely spot on the left between an old building and a grange. Find the red loop trail behind the buildings.

The Lisha Kill Natural Area hides an unexpected enclave of hemlocks and eastern old growth at the urban edge of Schenectady.

Watkins Glen State Park

Watkins Glen is best known for its flume-like whitewater and falls, but the park could have equal prestige for its hemlocks and hardwoods shading the rocky chasm—a top tourist attraction of the Finger Lakes region.

Pavement and boardwalks run 2 miles through the gorge with 400 feet of gradient stepping down 19 waterfalls. Along the busy arterial path are miniature but ancient hemlocks and yellow birches sparely rooted in cliff cracks. But leave all that behind: the big trees and wild forests rise at the upstream end of the park on woodland trails reached by ascending the gorge or more directly by parking beyond the main trailheads after you drive in from the entrance. Start with a park map at the visitor center.

Spring, summer, and fall are good. Watkins Glen attracts worldwide tourists—busloads—plus spillover from a loud auto racetrack nearby, so it's best to visit early in the day or after summer's crunch.

From Elmira, drive north on Route 14 to the southern end of the town of Watkins Glen and turn west into the park.

LOCATION
north of Corning

LENGTH
2 miles

DIFFICULTY
easy to moderate

TREE SPECIES
hemlocks, sweet birches, sugar maples, striped maples, northern red oaks, white pines

HIGHLIGHTS
virgin hemlocks and hardwoods, wooded waterfalls and gorge

Upstream from the popular gorge at Watkins Glen, a grove of ancient hemlocks shades steep slopes while beech trees green the understory.

Allegany State Park

LOCATION
south of Buffalo and
Salamanca

LENGTH
1 mile

DIFFICULTY
moderate

TREE SPECIES
black cherries, beeches,
hemlocks, sugar maples,
northern red oaks

HIGHLIGHTS
old black cherries, hemlocks,
hardwoods

In one of the finer old-growth groves
of the Northeast, sugar maples,
oaks, and maples can be seen in
Allegany State Park. Wild black
cherries, on the far left, thrive here.
Crafted into furniture, black cherry
is the most sought-after wood in the
East. Conservationists saved these
trees after a prolonged battle over
the aged grove.

Unlike other woodland walks in this book, this one
has no trail, but walking is easy, and the old trees are
magnificent.

Allegany State Park (don't confuse it with
Allegheny National Forest nearby in Pennsylvania)
is most used at its swimming beach, but the Big
Basin of 400 acres harbors ancient forests with one
of the East's best places to see wild black cherry
trees up to 50 inches across. Other hardwoods date
to 350 years. Basswoods, red maples, and white
pines make for a diverse community.

This is one of the "driftless" areas in New York
that escaped glaciation in the Wisconsin Ice Age,
leaving an uninterrupted genetic record of continuous forest growth and a roll call of species,
including some—such as cucumber magnolia—
found mainly southward.

In 1981, the state announced plans to log the entire area, leading to a largely successful 14-year
defense campaign. Like other forests of the Northeast,
deer overbrowsing, beech bark disease, and the hemlock woolly adelgid have taken their tolls, and the
future is even more uncertain with exotic pests such
as the emerald ash borer.

Snow piles up here downwind of the Great
Lakes, making off-trail tramping difficult in winter.
Autumn is awesome.

From I-86/Highway 17 southeast of Salamanca,
use exit 19 and follow signs south to Allegany State
Park, Red House Lake, and the headquarters. Take
Park Road 2 along the lake a quarter mile, turn right
on Park Road 1, go 2 miles, pull off at the first stone
bridge, and stroll upstream. Bushwhack downstream
for more big trees. If venturing far from the road, take
a compass for this flat, view-impaired terrain.

APPALACHIAN MOUNTAINS AND PIEDMONT

Standing on a rock outcrop almost anywhere along the crest of the Appalachian Mountains one can view a seemingly endless parade of ridges, rounded summits, and rolling plateaus, all covered with trees.

The backbone of the Appalachians totals 1,550 linear miles in the United States, plus more in Canada, but for this book I included the mountains north of Pennsylvania as part of New England because of their distinctive topography and legacy of glaciation. From the New York-Pennsylvania line to Alabama, this undulating terrain constitutes America's greenest empire of trees and the most diverse mixture of vascular plant species on the continent.

Mountaintops, shaded gorges, and north aspects with chilled microclimates harbor elegant northern hardwoods—maple, beech, and birch. In most of the Appalachians, central hardwoods dominate in variety that's often taken for granted, especially by people like me who grew up there. The Appalachians feature more than 100 tree species, completely covering the mountains and hills except for farmed fields, roads, towns, mowed lawns, and occasional outcrops of ancient sandstone cherished for their open vistas to—of course—more trees.

Beyond the mountainous Appalachian terrain that climbs with gradient varying from a few hundred to 4,000 feet at a single pitch, this forest community ramps down eastward to merge with the gentler Piedmont Province, which in turn stairsteps to sea level on the Atlantic Coastal Plain. Appalachian forests also reach westward from the range's backbone, angling down across plateaus deeply incised by rivers and onward to low elevations of the Midwest. Together, the Appalachian Mountains and related Piedmont nourish America's largest forest biome.

Spared the glacial interruptions that periodically wiped clean the woodland slate farther north, forests here evolved through millennia with the freedom to interbreed, adapt, mutate, and isolate into distinctive pockets of habitat, all leading to an evolutionary hotbed of diversity that the distinguished botanist Lucy Braun credited as the seed source of other forests beyond. A subgroup called Cove Hardwoods, in the Smoky Mountains, ranks as an exemplar with 130 tree species, 1,400 flowering herbs, and 2,000 varieties of fungi. Though precious few remain, fantastically large trees can be found there: black cherry boles six feet in diameter and red oaks 170 feet tall, to name just two.

Up to 40 species of trees can be found in a single acre in the southern Appalachians, while 10 or more per acre are common throughout much of the range. Compare this to Wyoming, a beautiful state but one with only a dozen tree species across an expanse that takes six hours of nonstop driving to cross. Dominant in the Appalachians are 10 kinds of oaks, five maples, four hickories, more willows than any amateur can identify, and pockets of conifers including elegant white pines historically topping 200 feet—approaching in height many of the tall conifers of the West Coast.

Once crowning the Appalachians, chestnuts as fat as 17 feet in diameter produced prolific crops of protein-rich nuts that fed entire ecosystems. Tragically, adult chestnuts were virtually all killed by an exotic fungus in the early 1900s, leaving only sapling-sized root sprouts that continue to regerminate, keeping alive the hope for recovery in cross-breeding efforts. Other hardwoods thrived in the breech, and, as often happens, visitors today lack knowledge or memory of the rich baseline of chestnut forest that once reigned.

Favorites here include a cast of still-charismatic broadleaf trees. High on the list, tulip trees (or tulip "poplars," though they are not in the poplar family) grow fast with tulip-shaped leaves, large springtime flowers for which the tree was named, and boles aiming straight for the sky. They are now the most common of the forest giants, reaching 190 feet. Absent the chestnuts, tulip trees have become a visual champion of eastern forests. But not to downplay sugar maples, beeches, northern red oaks, white oaks, basswoods, shagbark hickories, and sycamores, plus the intimate beauty of birches, hornbeams, smaller maple and oak species, and utterly elegant flowering dogwoods, which are also beset by an exotic blight.

Hikers in the Appalachians can choose among hundreds—actually thousands—of paths to see all of this beauty. The Appalachian Trail, maintained for nearly 2,200 miles from Maine to Georgia, runs along the range's northeast-southwest axis. Side trails and myriad other routes visit intriguing waterfalls, grassy balds, dark hollows, and woodlands variable in every respect. Eight national forests and two national parks—Shenandoah and Great Smoky Mountains—welcome walkers.

Though gray, and often with a biting cold dampness, winter in this region offers hiking at lower and southern elevations less prone to snow and ice. In springtime, nothing quite compares to the bursting greenery and sweet-scented blooming vibrancy of the Appalachian forest. During the summer, count on a welcome balminess if not humid heat. Autumn's cooler days and color, with their woodland beauty and delight, rival that of New England.

Salt Springs State Park

PENNSYLVANIA

LOCATION
north of Scranton, west of
New Milford

LENGTH
1-mile out and back or loop

DIFFICULTY
easy to moderate

TREE SPECIES
hemlocks

HIGHLIGHTS
hemlock gorge, cascading
stream

PREVIOUS SPREAD: In autumn, birches,
sycamores, and beeches glow with
warm colors along Slippery Rock Creek
at McConnells Mill State Park
in Pennsylvania.

Birches, striped maples, and hemlocks
shade the rocky edges of Fall Brook in
Salt Springs State Park.

FOLLOWING SPREAD: The steep slopes
above cascading Fall Brook are home to
an excellent grove of eastern hemlocks.

Pennsylvania is literally "Penn's Woods," named after the state's heroic Quaker founder, William Penn, whose 1681 edict proclaimed that one in five acres of forest be spared the axe. He didn't know that, over the next two centuries, successors to his utopia for religious freedom would raze not just 80 but 99.9 percent of the primeval forest in the heart of what was once an Appalachian paradise. Only a handful of small reserves remain as virgin forests through courageous efforts of tree lovers. Other selected groves and forest parks are recovering with native qualities that are beginning to reappear.

Salt Springs State Park is one of these reserves with both ancient trees and recovering forest. Near the New York border, this woodland darkens on steep slopes veering down to Fall Brook and its bubbly pitch over horizontal shelves of sandstone. If the onslaught of the hemlock woolly adelgid can be resisted, this grove will remain one of the finer surviving examples of ancient conifers south of New England. Old-growth analysts Bruce Kershner and Robert T. Leverett found 440-year-old hemlocks here and speculated that 700-year-old trees were possible.

All seasons are open for a visit, with winter having its own charms and challenges, namely treacherous ice.

From I-81 north of Scranton, drive to New Milford's exit 223 and turn west on Route 706. Drive toward Montrose, go north on Route 29 for 7 miles, and then turn west on State Route 4008 to the park on the left. Walk upstream, or, for prime hemlocks, cross Fall Brook's footbridge and climb steeply for an unusual perspective down into the canopy of conifers rooted in the ravine.

Ricketts Glen State Park

PENNSYLVANIA

LOCATION
east of Williamsport,
west of Scranton

LENGTH
3 miles as a prime loop,
7 miles in all

DIFFICULTY
moderate to strenuous

PRIMARY TREES
sugar maples, beeches,
hemlocks, white pines, tulip
trees, northern red oaks,
white oaks, yellow birches

HIGHLIGHTS
waterfalls in the woods

An Appalachian wonderland, this refuge centers around a pair of streams cascading down 22 waterfalls shaded by hardwoods and hemlocks, all seen from stairsteps built by the Civilian Conservation Corps with stone-mason artistry in the 1930s.

At 13,050 acres, this is one of Pennsylvania's largest state parks; it includes 2,000 acres of unlogged forest within Glens Natural Area, a national natural landmark. Though long dead, the oldest recorded eastern hemlock grew here for 988 years—far longer than any living hemlock today and longer than almost any other trees in the East except baldcypresses, which are in a class by themselves.

The trail system loops up one tributary of Kitchen Creek and down the other with the primary 3-mile route using the Highland, Glen Leigh, and Ganoga Glen Trails. Hikers can appreciate tulip trees up to 127 feet tall, hemlocks at 118 feet, comparable white pines, and tall mixed hardwoods.

From I-80 exit 236 at Bloomsburg, go north on Route 487, avoid myriad turnoffs, and continue to the state park.

One of 22 wooded waterfalls at Ricketts Glen State Park splashes down among hemlocks and sweet birches crowding stairsteps of the state park trail.

OPPOSITE: Fallen leaves of sugar maples, beeches, and sweet birches decorate boulders and bedrock during a soaking rainfall at Ricketts Glen.

Alan Seeger Natural Area

PENNSYLVANIA

LOCATION
southeast of State College

LENGTH
1 mile

DIFFICULTY
easy

TREE SPECIES
hemlocks, tulip trees, red maples, beeches, yellow and black birches, black gums, white pines, pignut hickories, white oaks, northern red oaks, chestnut oaks, rhododendrons

HIGHLIGHTS
ancient hemlocks, large white pines, hardwoods

Among the East's classic old-growth forests, this out-of-the-way 120-acre refuge is credited as the oldest in the Northeast by Kershner and Leverett, with hemlocks dating to 600 years old according to a ring count on a fallen giant. Knowing where to lavish praise, botanist Lucy Braun called this tract "a perfect example of a hemlock forest." Woolly adelgid infestations have left trees prone and rotting, but others are being treated by state forest managers with hopes of sustaining the landmark grove. Tulip trees reach 138 feet, and other hardwoods compete.

In 1921 this was one of the first groves in the Northeast set aside for its virgin trees, which had amazingly survived given that roads and a logging railroad led virtually to the site for years prior.

A loop trail weaves through the dense forest with rhododendrons 20 feet tall blossoming outrageously pink in June. The preserve is open all year, but the gravel roads get rutted with snow in winter. Alan Seeger Natural Area is a highlight of the 328-mile-long Mid State Trail running north-south through Pennsylvania—the vision and legacy of the Keystone State's trails enthusiast and hero of this hiking route, Tom Thwaites.

From State College—home of Penn State University—drive east on Highway 322. Just beyond Boalsburg, turn south on Bear Meadows Road. Continue on it by jogging left at Wampler Road and driving 1 mile, then turn right, and finally turn left on Stone Creek Road to Seeger Road.

Hemlocks of the Alan Seeger Natural Area survive in Rothrock State Forest. Guidebook authors Bruce Kershner and Robert T. Leverett called this the "oldest big-tree forest in the Northeast" and cited it as one of the first groves to be set aside for protection.

Minister Creek, Allegheny National Forest

LOCATION
south of Warren

LENGTH
7-mile loop; shorter out-and-back options

DIFFICULTY
moderate to strenuous

TREE SPECIES
white pines, hemlocks, hardwoods

HIGHLIGHTS
riparian forest, mixed hardwoods

Near the center of Allegheny National Forest, Minister Creek is a recovering watershed with captivating hemlock bottoms, beech and hardwood groves, and diverse plant life of the Allegheny Plateau, which comprises the west slope of the Appalachian chain through northern and western Pennsylvania—a topographic province accounting for nearly half the 370-mile-wide state.

This national forest of 513,000 acres is one of three in the Northeast, but it has been painfully compromised by logging and more egregiously by widespread industrial ownership of mineral rights. When the national forest was cobbled together through acquisitions of private land in 1923, many previous owners retained title to underground rights. Those rights typically found their way into the hands of coal and gas companies, whose mining and drilling take precedence over rights of surface ownership, which can be severely degraded in the extraction process. That makes Minister Creek and a few other intact areas all the more precious in a region where commodity production typically rules.

The trail starts at a campground and treads through a shaded community of hemlocks, white pines, and northern hardwoods, sometimes following abandoned railroad grades. The forest shows the ability of eastern woodlands to recover when given a chance, though the process is still underway.

This region is one of the best for wild black cherry trees, which germinated in sunlit openings after original old growth was cut and burned, and which now grow to impressive heights. The trail

A fern called rock polypody colonizes cracks in the sedimentary layers of sandstone cliffs above Minister Creek.

tours formidable rock formations and loops back to the campground.

From Warren, take Highway 6 south 5 miles to Weldbank and turn west on Cherry Grove Road. Continue south on Minister Road, go west on Route 666, and immediately angle right into Minister Creek's parking lot.

Often cited in forest literature, the Hearts Content and Tionesta Natural Areas of Allegheny National Forest were long regarded among the finest old-growth reserves in the East, and I treasure vivid memories of them from the 1970s. Unfortunately, my recent visits found hemlock die-off from woolly adelgid, widespread ravages of beech bark disease, and overbrowsing by deer. All this has opened the canopy and made it vulnerable to windthrow and further transitions to entangled brush, though some old white pines and hardwoods can still be found.

Woodlands of Allegheny National Forest shade the intimate trout waters of Minister Creek. Hemlocks and beeches line the stream while wild cherries and other hardwoods thrive above.

Cook Forest State Park

Morning sun warms the corrugated bark of a hemlock in Cook Forest State Park.

OPPOSITE: Taken together, the white pines, hemlocks, and hardwoods of Cook Forest are considered the tallest grove in the greater Northeast. In this photo a white pine stands shadowed in the center while hemlocks and beeches rise beside the Longfellow Trail.

Credited with the tallest overall assemblage of white pines and hemlocks in the East, the 8,500-acre Cook Forest State Park includes 2,353 acres of aged trees up to 470 years old. For decades, the East's tallest tree north of the Smoky Mountains was the 185-foot Longfellow Pine, but it and several other giants blew down in 2018. Surviving pines top 170 feet. Hemlocks reach 148 feet, and hardwoods also excel.

The park's story is a fabled tale of protection, even if too little, too late in retrospect. Timber baron Anthony Wayne Cook recognized the groves here as exceptional and set them aside from his own

company's cutting, eventually garnering the support needed to make the tract a state park in 1928—one of the nation's first reserves set aside explicitly to protect an ancient forest. The Forest Cathedral grove is now a registered national natural landmark.

Periodic windstorms uproot and tumble big trees—2017 and 2018 both saw crushing losses. Every tree that falls makes others more exposed to future windthrow—all reinforcing the importance of protecting large tracts of forest rather than just small acreage exposed to "edge effect" from wind and other hazards, including those as subtle as crow depredations of songbird eggs that otherwise remain hidden amid thick canopies.

The hemlock woolly adelgid is also infesting Cook Forest, but insightful park managers are diligently treating several thousand trees with insecticide, hoping to forestall the demise of the finest groves until biological predators to the adelgid become established. The Cook Forest Conservancy and Friends of Cook Forest work to support state efforts aimed at saving the signature trees.

Though damaged and threatened, Cook Forest remains a remarkable preserve. Trails traverse all the major groves. Topping the list, the Longfellow Trail loops through hemlocks and the Forest Cathedral grove of white pines, including the fallen Longfellow. With a map from the visitor center, see also the Hemlock and Seneca Trails.

Hiking is excellent year-round, with snow intermittent through winter. Springtime has a dreamy sweetness to it. Go on weekdays to avoid crowds in summer and when fall colors peak.

From I-80 exit 78 west of Brookville, take Route 36 north, cross the Clarion River, turn right, and park at the visitor center.

McConnells Mill
State Park

PENNSYLVANIA

LOCATION
north of Pittsburgh, south of
Slippery Rock

LENGTH
2-mile loop

DIFFICULTY
easy

TREE SPECIES
beeches, hemlocks, sweet
birches, maples

HIGHLIGHTS
classic hemlock gorge with
boulders and whitewater

At McConnells Mill State Park, a
December snowstorm whitens
needles of hemlocks and the
branches of sweet birches along
Slippery Rock Creek.

This 2,500-acre park covers both sides of Slippery
Rock Creek and symbolizes what may be the
most revered type of northeastern landscape: the
hemlock gorge. This one is classic, replete with
house-sized rocks, deep woods, foaming rapids, and
a tantalizing flavor of the primeval, if only localized.

The gorge was sculpted by runoff and melt-
water when glaciers forced streams into new
channels and successive ice-age lakes upstream
disgorged down the Slippery Rock channel with
explosive eroding power. Exceptional in a region
that has been thoroughly farmed and then merci-
lessly strip-mined for coal and further fragmented
by natural-gas fracking, this park is an oasis of
nature and a precious remnant of the wild.

From the historic grain mill, originally built in the
1800s and authentically redone, walk downstream
on a bedrock trail through dark hemlock groves and
past riverside boulders. After a mile, double back for
a completely different upstream perspective, or cross
the bridge and return on a more rugged trail. Another
path leads upstream from the mill.

Winter snow cover is iffy but a treat when you
find it. Spring and summer are beautiful, and fall has
gorgeous color with maples, birches, and beeches
that hold their amber leaves well into winter.

On I-79, go 40 miles north of Pittsburgh to exit
99, head west on Highway 422, pass the Highway
19 intersection, and turn south on McConnells Mill
Road. Four tight parking spots at the mill will likely be
filled, so don't even look unless you're a super-early
riser. Park as soon as you come to the large picnic
area perched on a high bench, and then descend to
the river on sandstone stairs among beeches and
other hardwoods—themselves worthy attractions.

Snow dusts the branches of hemlocks and rock polypody ferns along the McConnells Mill Trail.

OPPOSITE: A young beech tree clings to leaves that have turned from green to yellow and then amber as winter advances along Slippery Rock Creek.

Laurel Hill State Park

PENNSYLVANIA

LOCATION
west of Somerset

LENGTH
1-mile loop

DIFFICULTY
easy

TREE SPECIES
hemlocks, beeches, oaks, maples

HIGHLIGHTS
old hemlocks, hardwoods, stream

This small state park has a seven-acre grove of hemlocks up to 300 years old and 42 inches in diameter perched above Laurel Hill Creek.

From the Pennsylvania Turnpike's Somerset exit 110, head south on Route 601 into town, and go west on Route 31. In 7 miles, turn left at the state park sign. In another half mile, park before crossing the bridge. Walk across Laurel Hill Creek's bridge and go right on the Hemlock Trail. Soon turn left on the blue trail, climb, and then enter the ancient grove. At the next intersection, go right on the yellow trail to the largest hemlock.

Laurel Hill Creek reflects its forest at the height of autumn color.

OPPOSITE: Hemlocks and hardwoods rise in the small but exquisite grove at Laurel Hill State Park.

Ohiopyle State Park

PENNSYLVANIA

LOCATION
east of Uniontown

LENGTH
2 miles for Ferncliff Peninsula
Natural Area, plus other trails

DIFFICULTY
easy to moderate

TREE SPECIES
beeches, oaks, maples, tulip
trees, basswoods, hemlocks,
white pines, hickories

HIGHLIGHTS
diversity of hardwoods,
whitewater river

From Ohiopyle State Park's high
bridge crossing the Youghiogheny
River at the north end of the Ferncliff
Trail, hikers enjoy a rare view
downward into the top of the crown
of an Appalachian forest. This early
autumn medley features red maples
in red and green, tulip trees in yellow,
and chestnut oaks that are still green.

OPPOSITE: Magnificent beech trees
reach for the sky along Ohiopyle State
Park's Great Gorge Trail northbound
toward Kentuck Campground.
Beech bark disease is advancing
from the north and killing most large
beeches in its path. For now this
grove remains unaffected.

At 19,000 acres, Pennsylvania's most popular state
park is also one of the largest. An hour and a half
from Pittsburgh, its extraordinary attractions also
make it a popular destination from Washington, DC,
Baltimore, and Cleveland, each within four hours.

Traditionally the draw here was paddling, and
the Youghiogheny River remains one of the finest
and most popular whitewater kayaking, rafting, and
expert canoeing runs in America. In addition, a riverside railroad grade has been converted into a
bicycle trail attracting thousands on busy days,
all part of the Great Allegheny Passage and C & O
Canal Towpath, which is remarkably continuous for
335 miles from Pittsburgh to Washington, DC. The
forest here is fundamental to all these activities.

Midway in the Appalachian Range, this is a
meeting ground of tree species; oaks, maples, hemlocks, basswoods, and beeches crown the canopy.
For a stellar walk, go to Ferncliff Peninsula Natural
Area, a forest enclave on the inside of a distinctive 1.5-mile horseshoe bend of the Youghiogheny.
Recognized for its plant diversity and fine forest
even in the early 1900s era of unquestioned lum-
bering, this tract has been protected with its 15-acre
core of old growth among house-sized rocks and
steep frontage on the foaming river.

A starting point is the park visitor center near Ohiopyle Falls—among the largest waterfalls in the East by volume of flow. Park near there in the center of the Ohiopyle town site, and grab a map for the complex trail network.

To reach Ferncliff, drive or walk from Ohiopyle's main street (Route 381) to the north side of the river and turn west into the Ferncliff parking lot. A path leads to the river and heads downstream on the opposite side of the river from the town. Notice beautifully articulated carboniferous tree-fern fossils in the bedrock of the trail upstream from the falls. The clockwise loop then tours exquisite stands of mixed hardwoods and hemlocks of the peninsula formed by the sweeping U-shaped river bend. Favor routes that bear left, toward the river, for the full perimeter. An exceptional tulip tree and mixed hardwood grove lies at the north end of the loop near the base of the high pedestrian bridge across the Youghiogheny River (west of the other bike-trail bridge back in the town of Ohiopyle). Bear right to complete the loop back to Ferncliff's parking lot.

For more forest hiking after the loop, instead of returning to the Ferncliff lot, walk left, cross the high bridge (an attraction in its own right), and immediately take the Great Gorge Trail left (southbound and upstream, with the river on your left). This leads in a mile to the tributary Cucumber Falls amid old trees, with a connecting trail to Ohiopyle, the visitor center, and the Ferncliff lot.

For a criterion beech forest, cross the high bridge at the northwest (downstream) end of the Ferncliff loop trail, walk downriver on the bike trail past the initial left turn of the Great Gorge Trail (southbound), and in a short distance take the next trail left, the Great Gorge Trail (northbound). Head up the mountain toward the Kentuck Trail for half a mile into one of the finer beech groves I've ever seen. As of this writing, it is unaffected by beech bark disease, though the elegant trees' days may be numbered.

Another forest walk explores Meadow Run; from Ohiopyle Falls, walk downriver along the

highway, cross Meadow Run, and take the trail up the scenic bedrock stream.

Spring, summer, and fall are good, with delightful swimming in the hot months. Weekdays and early mornings are best at this busy park. Evening strolls are enchanting when sweet scents of the Appalachian summer infuse everything.

On the Pennsylvania Turnpike east of Pittsburgh, use Donegal exit 91 and follow Route 31 east for 2 miles. At Route 711, turn right, go south 10 miles, turn left at Route 381, and continue 11 miles to Ohiopyle. Just before the bridge over the Youghiogheny River, at the Wilderness Voyageurs Outfitters store on the left, turn right into the Ferncliff lot, or cross the river and park in the big lot near the falls.

OPPOSITE: The trail up Meadow Run is one of many woodland wonders in Ohiopyle State Park. Here, near the Route 381 bridge, sweet birches and white oaks have dropped their leaves on bedrock while rhododendrons and hemlocks green the banks.

Glossy after a summer thunderstorm, a young beech shines along the bedrock edge of Meadow Run's steep flume near the Youghiogheny River in Ohiopyle State Park.

Bull's Island Recreation Area

NEW JERSEY

LOCATION
northwest of Trenton

LENGTH
1 mile

DIFFICULTY
easy

TREE SPECIES
tulip trees, sycamores, silver maples, beeches, oaks

HIGHLIGHTS
undisturbed floodplain forest

Though densely developed, New Jersey has a number of remarkable small preserved forests, and some include big trees in the mild climate of the mid-Atlantic coast. Bull's Island is one of these hidden surprises.

This rare assemblage of old growth in a 42-acre natural area includes sycamores, tulip trees, silver maples, and aged grape vines fat as twisted tree trunks. A trail loops through the forest strip sandwiched on the island between the Delaware River and the Delaware and Raritan Canal. Somehow escaping the cut from colonial times onward, the island and a stretch of the canal were made a state park in 1974. Visit any month of the year.

The site lies directly across the Delaware River from Lumberville, Pennsylvania, and north of Stockton, New Jersey. From Highway 202 going east from Pennsylvania, cross the Delaware to Lambertville, New Jersey, and turn north on Route 29. Go 3 miles to Stockton, continue 3 miles on Route 29, and turn left onto Bull's Island. Walk to the west side of the canal and the loop trail to the island's south end. A footbridge across the Delaware to Lumberville offers a nice view and makes the island accessible to hikers from the Pennsylvania side.

Along the lower Delaware River, tulip trees, beeches, and oaks on Bull's Island survived logging and canal construction. Sycamores and silver maples also tower over this wedge of land between the river and the Delaware and Raritan Canal. A mature tulip tree, right of center, steals the show in this photo.

Stephens State Park

NEW JERSEY

LOCATION
east of Hackettstown

LENGTH
2 miles out and back

DIFFICULTY
easy

TREE SPECIES
sycamores, silver maples, beeches, ironwoods (also called American hornbeams)

HIGHLIGHTS
floodplain forest, large silver maples

Ironwood trees, known for muscular sinews in their trunks, edge the Musconetcong River in Stephens State Park. Birds and squirrels relish the fruits of this small tree.

OPPOSITE: Silver maples shade the banks of the Musconetcong River. The most common riparian tree in the East and Midwest, these maples with deeply cut leaves grow fast. Prone to breakage in storms and floods, limbs and trunks fall into the streams and further enrich aquatic ecosystems by providing habitat and cover for fish and invertebrates.

The Musconetcong River is little known beyond its region, but at the 805-acre Stephens State Park, just north of Hackettstown, a well-worn path leads upriver through a floodplain forest of large silver maples, beeches, and other riparian trees. This is a national wild and scenic river with swimming, canoeing, and fishing in one of the state's better trout streams.

From Highway 46 going east through Hackettstown, turn north on Willow Grove Street before crossing the river and follow signs to the park. Walk up the southeast bank.

Swallow Falls State Park

MARYLAND

LOCATION
9 miles north of Oakland

LENGTH
1.3-mile loop

DIFFICULTY
easy

TREE SPECIES
hemlocks, sugar maples, beeches, sweet birches

HIGHLIGHTS
forested riverfront and falls, old hemlocks, rhododendron thickets

This park is known for its five waterfalls, with the largest one on the Youghiogheny River (much smaller than the falls far downstream at Ohiopyle), but the park is equally exceptional for its forest. The last ancient grove of its size in Maryland is composed of mixed hardwoods and hemlocks aged to 300 years.

From the main parking lot and visitor center, walk the loop clockwise, first to the 53-foot Muddy Creek Falls, then to Swallow Falls of the Youghiogheny. Notice the fine old growth throughout the river bottom and near the main falls.

From I-68 exit 4 at Friendsville, go south on Route 42 to Highway 219. Continue south on Highway 219 for 5 miles to Thayerville. One mile beyond, turn west and follow signs on back roads to Swallow Falls Road and the park.

At Swallow Falls State Park, hemlocks and northern hardwoods occupy the shores of the Youghiogheny River near its headwaters. Roots of sweet birch probe for sustenance around cracks of boulders, and a few shoots of dog hobble—impenetrably thick across much of its range farther south in the Appalachians—sprout in the foreground. The park features one of the finest remaining groves of hemlocks this far south.

Patapsco Valley State Park

MARYLAND

LOCATION
southwest of Baltimore

LENGTH
3-mile loop, options for less or more

DIFFICULTY
easy to moderate

TREE SPECIES
tulip trees, oaks, sugar maples, beeches, basswoods, sycamores

HIGHLIGHTS
deep deciduous forest, large beech and tulip trees

Spectacular woodland trails wind through ravines that lead down to the Patapsco River. Unlike most trees with rough bark that cracks to expand as the living layer beneath it grows, beech trees maintain silvery bark that stays smooth because it remains alive and grows in tandem with the cambium inside. Tulip trees, with darker, vertically cracked bark, crown the canopy.

Patapsco Valley State Park's deciduous forest of big trees is surrounded by suburbanizing neighborhoods just 10 miles from Baltimore and 50 miles north of Washington, DC. This was Maryland's first state park and among the earliest in the country; a modest donation of land in 1907 has grown to 16,000 acres.

A superb greenway stretches with only a few interruptions for 32 miles along this tributary to Chesapeake Bay. The section featured here lies downstream from Ellicott City, where three dams have been removed in recent years, restoring the Patapsco River to natural flows and migration of shad, herring, and eels.

From the Cascade Trailhead along the river, walk south and uphill into the splendid hardwood forest. Other loops and 200 miles of park trails offer fine woodland groves. Unfortunately, exotic wavy-leaf basketgrass spreads epidemically across this park and whole mid-Atlantic states with no remedy in sight.

Hiking is fine all year with typically mild winters. Spring and fall are outstanding; summer days are often hot and humid.

While the fine beech, tulip tree, and hardwood forest can be reached by access points including a riverbank trail south of Ellicott City, and from Landing Road in a rural neighborhood south of the river, the clearest approach is from downstream. On I-95 take exit 47 (first exit north of the Patapsco), ramp onto I-195 south, exit immediately onto busy Highway 1 southbound, and soon turn right onto South Street, marked with a sign for the park. Drive upstream, cross the river on Gun Road, and go 1.6 miles to the Cascade Trail, on the left at a parking lot near Swinging Bridge.

Rock Creek Park

LOCATION
Northwest DC

LENGTH
1 mile or more, out and
back or loops

DIFFICULTY
easy

TREE SPECIES
tulip trees, oaks, maples,
basswoods, hickories, beeches

HIGHLIGHTS
deciduous forest, large beech
and tulip trees

Lost to many in the lineup of monuments and museums of the nation's capital, Rock Creek Park was historically the third unit of the national park system, created by Congress in 1890, predating even Yosemite (Yellowstone and Mackinac came first, but Mackinac was decommissioned in 1895).

Woodlands in this 1,800-acre public estate might be regarded as a prime example of a semiwild greenway at a scale found in few other cities. Dozens of species of trees thrive in the temperate climate of hot summers.

Miles of trail loop, link, and wander through the linear park, all accessible by public transit within a few blocks from park boundaries. My first walks here were primeval escapes from the bounds of Georgetown University, a mile away, when I was enrolled there in the 1960s. Main trails are traveled at all times; my recent sunrise pilgrimage for photos was shared with joggers even in the faint light of daybreak. Some runners and bicyclists are lucky enough to commute to work on trails and streets here. On weekends, Park Service rangers lead

Thousands of people enjoy the trails of Rock Creek Park daily, but quiet retreats and woodland byways await within this urban forest.

OPPOSITE: Rock Creek Park showcases an urban forest. Here above Bingham Drive—closed to cars—the striated bark of tulip trees reaches high and the mottled bark of a sycamore rises on the right while sugar maples, basswoods, and oaks compete for sunlight.

In Rock Creek Park off Bingham Drive, the curved trunks of sycamores catch sunlight at daybreak while a tulip tree remains shaded beneath the canopy.

OPPOSITE: Near Oregon and Nebraska Avenues in Rock Creek Park, a tulip tree is backed by sugar maples, red oaks, and basswoods in early morning light.

guided nature walks, and some of the streets are closed to make open space even more amenable to walkers and bicyclists.

Fine groves of big trees straddle the now-closed-to-traffic Bingham Drive, off the intersection of Oregon and Nebraska Avenues on the west side, midway down the length of the park.

The 10-mile-long greenway can be accessed virtually anywhere along its northeast-southwest alignment, including many points off 16th Street on the east side and at Oregon Avenue and other west-side streets. The DC-Chevy Chase boundary lies northward, and the park continues upstream through Montgomery County, Maryland, for another 14 miles. Beach Drive and adjacent bike paths approximate a centerline of the park through Washington.

Cathedral State Park

LOCATION
northeastern West Virginia

LENGTH
3 miles, with shorter loops

DIFFICULTY
easy

TREE SPECIES
hemlocks, sugar maples, beeches, sweet birches

HIGHLIGHTS
West Virginia's largest old-growth forest

This forest is West Virginia's only remaining virgin hemlock grove and largest tract of old growth, though it's only 132 acres in a state of 15 million acres with 352,000 acres of strip mines decapitating 135 mountains. But, as an unexpected gem near the edge of Appalachia's coal country, trees 90 feet tall are a sample of the forest that once typified cool microclimates throughout the middle Appalachians. This oasis of nature supports 170 species of trees, ferns, and wildflowers.

The entire trail network is worth the walk, especially the Giant Hemlock and Cathedral Trails, spring through fall.

From Oakland in western Maryland, drive south on Highway 219, go west on Highway 50, and in a few miles turn right into the park.

In classic combination, a hemlock and rhododendron share the stage in a forest of eastern hornbeams, sweet birches, and beeches at Cathedral State Park.

OPPOSITE: Scarlet leaves of autumn's sour gum (also called black gum or black tupelo) splash their color across the trunks of two great hemlocks at Cathedral State Park, the state's finest remnant of old-growth Appalachian forest.

Blackwater Falls
State Park

LOCATION
Davis, northern Monongahela
National Forest

LENGTH
1 mile, with longer options

DIFFICULTY
moderate to strenuous

TREE SPECIES
hemlocks, beeches, sweet
birches, maples, oaks

HIGHLIGHTS
deep woods along a rocky river,
forested mountain views

At Blackwater Falls State Park,
the Lindy Point Trail leads to a
gleaming outcrop of quartz-rich
sandstone overlooking a wooded
empire of the park and also
Monongahela National Forest. Red
maples begin turning in autumn
color among mixed hardwoods of
the Appalachian Plateau, incised
here by the Blackwater River.

FOLLOWING SPREAD: A showcase of
nature, Blackwater Falls cascades
among hemlocks, birches, beeches,
and rhododendrons.

Blackwater Falls State Park highlights West Virginia's eastern mountains—largely unspoiled by coal mining and lacking the blasted summits and fluorescent-orange acid-mine drainage too often found elsewhere in the state.

Hemlocks, red spruces, white pines, birches, and mixed hardwoods shade sandstone ledges of the 57-foot waterfall and its tumult of boulder-riddled rapids below. A paved path descends 200 steps to an overlook.

Other trails explore 20 miles of ridges, canyon rims, and streamfronts, including a half-mile path to Lindy Point, with its enthralling view from bleached quartzite to wooded horizons. Drive past the park lodge and sledding hill and watch for the trailhead on the right before the road narrows.

Spring, summer, and fall are excellent. This outpost of the Appalachian Plateau turns shockingly arctic in winter, but with attention to slippery ice, views of the falls and its forest are amazing then. Easier trails are open for cross-country skiing.

From the southwestern corner of Maryland, drive Highway 219 south to the crossroads of Thomas, go east on Route 32 to Davis, and turn right on Blackwater Falls Road. Take the stairway to the falls, and explore surrounding uplands with a map from the visitor center.

Just a few miles south on Route 32, the unique Appalachian landscape of Canaan Valley National Wildlife Refuge features red spruces lingering since ice-age recovery, plus artistic arrangements of acid-loving bog vegetation: Labrador tea, azalea, and rhododendron.

Montpelier Forest

VIRGINIA

LOCATION
northeast of Charlottesville

LENGTH
1- to 2-mile loop

DIFFICULTY
easy

TREE SPECIES
tulip trees, pawpaws, white oaks, beeches

HIGHLIGHTS
large tulip trees, pawpaws

This estate of America's fourth president, James Madison, is also a splendid deciduous forest with trees 150 years old thriving in a climate of short winters and long, humid growing seasons. Though little known elsewhere, this is one of my favorite mature deciduous forests that's easily reached in the southern Appalachians. Monticello, the celebrated Thomas Jefferson estate, lies nearby for history buffs interested in both presidents.

Tulip trees and other hardwoods grow tall at Montpelier. Uncommon north of Virginia but robust here, pawpaws with wide-tipped leaves crowd the understory and produce fruits favored by many mammals and also used in traditional southern desserts such as pawpaw pudding.

Though private, 8 miles of trail on 1,024 acres are protected by a conservation easement and generously open to the public. For big trees, take the Poplar Run and Spicebush Loops at the southern end. Drive south on the entrance road, park on the right near the Madison house, and walk south to the trailhead, or continue to limited parking off Farm Road at the southern apex of the loop road. Outdoor visitors do not have to pay for the house tour; hike for free, though the tour is worthwhile.

Springtime brings birdsongs and autumn days brighten with color, and it's not too hot then. Early summer mornings can be magically humid and quiet except for welcome birdsongs; be there when the gate opens at 9:00 a.m. to beat the heat.

From the north side of Charlottesville, drive east on the Highway 250 bypass. Take Route 20 north, avoid turnoffs, and continue to Montpelier's entrance on the right, 3 miles before the mini-burg of Orange.

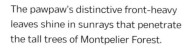

The pawpaw's distinctive front-heavy leaves shine in sunrays that penetrate the tall trees of Montpelier Forest.

OPPOSITE: Montpelier, the estate of President James Madison, is home to one of the finest mature hardwood forests in the Piedmont Province— a foothills and flattened region covering the Eastern Seaboard from the base of the Appalachians to the Coastal Plain. Here tulip trees take their usual stand with the highest canopy in a forest still recovering from the loss of the American chestnut, which once dominated.

Whiteoak Canyon, Shenandoah National Park

LOCATION
southeast of Luray

LENGTH
5 miles or more, plus
connections to other trails

DIFFICULTY
strenuous

TREE SPECIES
white oaks, mixed hardwoods

HIGHLIGHTS
recovering forest, riparian
canyon, waterfalls

The Whiteoak Canyon Trail highlights
Shenandoah National Park and
illustrates the promise of forest recovery
from an earlier era of logging, burning,
and farming. Chestnut oaks and yellow
birches grow in this rocky fold of the
Blue Ridge Mountains.

Shenandoah National Park straddles the crest of the Blue Ridge Mountains—queen among Appalachian subranges, rising to 4,000 feet with a continuous profile for the 105-mile length of the park. At 196,000 acres, this is the largest protected landscape in mid-Appalachia. Skyline Drive tracks the crest and continues southward as the 469-mile Blue Ridge Parkway—America's longest linear park—to the Smoky Mountains of North Carolina and Tennessee. America's most-driven scenic mountain highway, Skyline Drive accesses dozens of hikes and 500 miles of trail.

Do not expect hoary old growth. Rather, this park is a demonstration of forests' ability to recover—or not—after clearing by farmers, loggers, and fire. Even with serial infestations of defoliating gypsy moths over the past few decades, the forest is a symbol of nature's ability to rebound if given a chance.

This hike is one of the park's finest, and the entire length to six waterfalls passes through hardwoods now approaching maturity. Not surprising, white oaks rise tall here, as do tulip trees and maples. The woolly adelgid killed all hemlocks early in the exotic insect's migration north, leaving a legacy of fallen trunks where deep shade had cooled the ground five decades ago when I first walked this path as a teenager. However, young hemlocks, treated with insecticide for now, can be seen near the beginning of the trail, offering hope that the great conifers of the past can one day be restored.

From Skyline Drive, take Whiteoak Canyon Trail and then walk east to charming streamfronts and deepening woods. At 86 feet high, Upper Whiteoak Falls makes for a 4.6-mile out and back,

or continue another 2.7 miles both ways for five more falls. In summer, think about the heat awaiting on the return—an aerobic workout of 1,100 vertical feet back up to the car.

Spring is intoxicating here, as is autumn, but beware: the popularity of fall-color weekends is over the top in this park easily reached by tens of millions. Hike on weekdays, or wait for the lingering oranges and ambers of early November. Winter is gray and icy but uncrowded; summer is hot.

To reach Whiteoak from Luray, take Highway 211 east to Skyline Drive and go south to milepost 42.5.

With more endurance and a map from the visitor center (milepost 51), continue down Whiteoak Canyon Trail and return on the more southerly Cedar Run Trail for a strenuous 7-mile jaunt—it seems way longer.

A real bang for the buck in hiking scenery lies just southward: at Skyline Drive's milepost 50.6, park and descend Dark Hollow Falls Trail to its ornate cataract—a steep 1.4-mile round trip. Back in the car, enjoy the entire Skyline Drive with strolls at repeated crossings of the Appalachian Trail, mostly through recovering chestnut oak forest.

OPPOSITE: The short but steep trail to Dark Hollow Falls awaits near Big Meadows, midway on the north-south drive through Shenandoah National Park. Yellow birches frame the ornate cascade.

The Appalachian forest matures in the depths of Whiteoak Canyon. Wild hydrangea green the foreground where hiker Jim Palmer pauses to admire the stream. Sugar maples, birches, and oaks rise beyond.

Great Smoky Mountains National Park

At Clingmans Dome in the Smoky Mountains, Fraser firs endure as relics from a colder climate during the last ice age. The sunset view here shows both dead snags and a resurrection of new trees. At 6,643 feet, this marks the highest point in Great Smoky Mountains National Park and the highest on the Appalachian Trail.

The Great Smoky Mountains are among the most legendary of ranges within the Appalachian chain, and the national park embracing them spans a 55-mile east-west crest straddling Tennessee to the north and North Carolina to the south. Owing to the Southeast's urban areas, this is the most-visited national park in the United States—12.5 million people visit annually—twice that of runner-up Grand Canyon National Park. The park's 522,000 acres are the second-largest protected forest in the East, behind only Adirondack Park, which is far more compromised with its mix of state and private land.

Though this rugged range claims some of the East's highest peaks, it's the forest more than the mountains that give the Smoky Mountains status as a landmark in American geography and as a UNESCO World Heritage Site. The range includes vertical relief from 875 to 6,643 feet undisturbed by ice-age glaciation. With intersecting life zones mixing the North, South, Coastal Plain, and Midwest, the Smokies shelter more biological diversity than any other mountains in the nation. Virgin forest covers 36 percent of the park—second only to the Adirondacks, though trees grow much larger here owing to the warmer climate. If one wants to see virtually all the tree species growing in the Appalachians—and the entire East except for Coastal Plain lowcountry and Florida subtropics—this is the place.

Rugged inaccessibility and arboreal productivity have also sheltered the largest number of "champion" trees—the largest individuals of their species. Most are obscurely remote, including the tallest hardwood in North America—a tulip tree

at 191.9 feet when last measured in 2011. The last 200-foot tree in the East was a Smoky Mountains white pine, measured at 207 feet in 1995, but it has since broken and was down to 188.9 feet in 2016.

Trails total 850 miles here. One can plot backpacking trips of 100 miles by linking some of the grandest groves together, as I once did by connecting eastern reaches of the park westward to Mount Le Conte and then north to Ramsey Prong. Easier day hikes beckon from road-accessible trailheads on all sides.

In the park's northeast corner, Albright Grove includes impressive tulip trees, oaks, and yellow buckeyes reached on an 18-mile loop from Cosby Campground via Gabes Mountain, Maddron Bald, and Snake Den Ridge Trails. Shorter, take a 6-mile out and back to the grove via Maddron Bald Trailhead; from Gatlinburg, Tennessee, drive east on Highway 73/321 for 15 miles and then go right on Baxter Road. In 0.4 miles, turn right into the Maddron lot. But don't leave your rig there overnight.

Ramsey Prong is a rugged stream in the northeastern part of the park reached from Greenbrier Road up the Little Pigeon River beyond the Greenbrier Ranger Station. See hardwoods along the 8-mile out and back to Ramsey Cascades.

At the Appalachian crest, both a road and the Appalachian Trail reach towering Clingmans Dome. A stand of rare Fraser firs endures there from colder climates that chilled high elevations during the Wisconsin Ice Age and spawned a biological legacy that lingers, confined to the highest terrain in North Carolina, Tennessee, and southern Virginia. Nearly eradicated in the 1970s and 1980s by the exotic balsam woolly adelgid, and poisoned

by air pollution from coal-burning power plants upwind in the Tennessee Valley, the firs now appear to be recovering as pollution regulations of the 1990s have gained traction. The firs' old snags along with new growth can be seen at the summit and its spiral-ramped viewing tower built to accommodate the crowds. Clingmans Dome Road dead-ends there, reached via Newfound Gap Road—the main highway bisecting the park south of Gatlinburg.

Consult with rangers and plan your Smoky Mountains hike in Park Service visitor centers at Sugarlands outside Gatlinburg or Oconaluftee at the southern end, or peruse Russ Manning's *100 Hikes in the Great Smoky Mountains*. Try shoulder seasons to avoid the crush of visitation. Get a permit well ahead of time and reserve campsites for backpacking.

OPPOSITE: In the Oconaluftee River valley of Great Smoky Mountains National Park, a yellow buckeye sapling stakes its claim at a sunlit meadow among blue phlox and mayapples.

Ramsey Prong bubbles from the rich temperate forest of the Smoky Mountains. This and other trails to remote locations in the national park hide both old-growth and recovering forests.

APPALACHIAN MOUNTAINS AND PIEDMONT

Joyce Kilmer Memorial Forest

Named for the poet of "Trees," this 3,800-acre natural area in Nantahala National Forest has long been recognized as a prized old-growth forest. A hundred tree species have been listed along the figure-eight trail; elders are 400 years old and 100 feet tall. Eastern hemlocks that only two decades ago made this grove a hushed cool refuge have all succumbed to the woolly adelgid. Dead snags were felled in 2010, and the site is drier and has much more sunlight than when I first visited in 1977.

To reach this remote area off the southwest corner of Great Smoky Mountains National Park, drive to Robbinsville and take Highway 129 north 1.5 miles. At Route 143 turn left, go 5 miles, and turn right on Kilmer Road. Continue 7.3 miles, staying right at the Santeetlah Gap/Cherohala Skyway intersection, and finally continue 2.5 more miles.

Don't confuse this eastern landmark with Joyce Kilmer Natural Area in central Pennsylvania—a nice but smaller 77 acres of white pines.

NORTH CAROLINA

LOCATION
south of Knoxville, Tennessee, and west of Robbinsville, North Carolina

LENGTH
2 miles

DIFFICULTY
easy

TREE SPECIES
tulip trees, yellow buckeyes, beeches, oaks, maples, sycamores, basswoods

HIGHLIGHTS
old-growth deciduous forest

At Joyce Kilmer Memorial Forest in Nantahala National Forest, tulip trees rise above the rest of the Appalachian woods, though the hemlocks that once darkened this monumental forest have been killed by invasions of an exotic insect, the hemlock woolly adelgid.

Savage Gulf State Natural Area

The name says it all, with summer hazards of ticks galore and rattlesnakes as a definite possibility. Savage Gulf is not for everyone. But it's a large refuge of big trees at the escarpment of the Cumberland Plateau—west of the core Appalachian uplift—and an arboreal highlight of Tennessee. The natural area supports many old hemlocks—8,000 being treated for the woolly adelgid. With 15,600 acres, this is one of the larger protected areas in the Southeast, also dedicated as a national natural landmark.

Near the park entrance, stop at the visitor center, get a map, and plot a route among 50 miles of trails in a maze of gorges cut into the plateau's tablelands. I've taken the North Rim Trail west to cliff tops, vistas, and the elegantly shaded waterfall of Savage Creek.

One can hike here all year, though if I had the choice I'd go back in autumn after most cold-blooded creatures have gone to sleep. Summer has the drawbacks mentioned previously.

From Chattanooga, take I-24 west and then go north on Route 28. At Whitwell, turn left on Route 108, bear right on Route 399 at Palmer, and turn left at the sign.

LOCATION
northwest of Chattanooga

LENGTH
2 miles or more

DIFFICULTY
moderate to strenuous

TREE SPECIES
hemlocks, oaks, hickories, tulip trees, Virginia and shortleaf pines

HIGHLIGHTS
hemlocks in the South, sandstone gorges

OPPOSITE: Oaks and hickories reign in the rugged wilds of Savage Gulf State Natural Area. Views from rock outcrops with Virginia pines reveal the hardwood expanse, which also includes a stronghold of large eastern hemlocks.

In the humid forest of Savage Gulf, this refreshing pool is irresistible on a hot summer day.

Red River Gorge Geological Area, Daniel Boone National Forest

KENTUCKY

LOCATION
southeast of Lexington

LENGTH
1 to 12 miles

DIFFICULTY
easy to moderate

TREE SPECIES
oaks, hickories, mixed hardwoods

HIGHLIGHTS
riparian hardwoods, sandstone arches

The Red River Gorge Geological Area of 29,000 acres has the largest assemblage of sandstone arches in the United States outside Arches National Park. Unlike that red-rock desert showcase, this one is thoroughly wooded, with a mingling of Appalachian hardwoods including oaks and hickories typical of lowlands transitioning into the Midwest, along with mature riparian broadleaves.

An Army Corps of Engineers dam would have flooded the finest forests along the Red River, but it was stopped by a citizens' movement in the 1970s and later sealed safe with a national wild and scenic river designation in 1993. The Clifty Wilderness of Daniel Boone National Forest, a national natural landmark, lies eastward.

To see the Red River hardwoods, go to the Sheltowee Connector Trail. The path leads upstream half a mile, crosses the river on a footbridge, then heads downstream with a connection to the Sheltowee Trace National Recreation Trail.

From I-64 east of Lexington, take exit 98 onto Combs Mountain Parkway. Take exit 33 at Slade, turn left, and then left again on Highway 15. Continue 1.5 miles, turn right on Route 77, and cross the Red River. Stay right on Route 715 going east, and continue 1.5 miles to the Sheltowee Connector Trail.

The striking leaves of a Fraser magnolia green the foreground while a cluster of sycamores dominates the background along the Red River near the Sheltowee Trace Trail.

OPPOSITE: Grays Arch looms above the oak and hickory forest where the Cumberland Plateau slants down from Appalachian highlands.

SOUTH

A special forest intrigue hovers around the moss-covered oaks, pinelands, swamps, and seashores of the southeastern United States. For this book, I define the South mostly as the Coastal Plain—the flat expanse nearing sea level in the Southeast through Florida and bordering the Gulf of Mexico. Because Georgia and Alabama are profoundly southern states, I also include their sections of the Piedmont and Appalachian Mountains.

The baldcypress is an arboreal centerpiece of the South. Oddly a deciduous conifer, growing cones but shedding needles in winter, these trees live longer than any others in the East—the record is 2,626 years! They reach enormous size in wetlands, responding to challenging habitat by sprouting "knees" as odd upshoots of roots that protrude above the water, and by bulking up with fluted bases that give a wider foundation for leveraged support in soil saturated with water.

Oaks are the largest genus of trees in the East, with most of the 42 species appearing in the South. Along with sycamores, Virginia live oaks, or simply live oaks, are the largest, eight feet across with crowns arcing 100 feet—giants in groves or growing alone. Adding eeriness, Spanish "moss"—actually a flowering epiphyte, *Tillandsia usneoides*—hangs by the bushel from branches of baldcypresses, oaks, and southern colleagues.

Forgotten by many owing to a long absence, longleaf pines—with cathedral-column boles and luxuriant 18-inch needles (think hair halfway down your back)—were once the keystone species across 92 million acres from Virginia to Texas. Logging took 98 percent, though it seems more like 100 percent; a single longleaf is difficult to find. At limited restoration plots, stewards varying from the Forest Service to quail-hunting clubs and a few dutiful inheritors of plantations aim to reestablish samples of what was arguably America's greatest pine forest.

Lightening the mood, sabal palms strike a subtropical pose at breezy coastal edges. Shrubby palmettos' fans of palmlike leaves speak to primeval jungle along the gulf, where you might imagine a seven-foot-long, yellow-eyed cougar silently appearing out of nowhere and watching your every move, which they once did.

Like elsewhere, forests here were logged to the limit, meaning every acre. We're left with a lot of farms and cities separated by second growth, third growth, and so on. Many tracts—hard to call them forests—are industrially mowed every 30 years. Loblolly and slash pines line up like corn in commercial plantations doused with herbicides and petrochemical fertilizer, harvested by the timber industry's version of a corn picker. How long this drain on soil, dearth of functioning ecosystems, and force-fed productivity can continue is a good question. Only a few pockets of woods date back a century, and a very few are older.

In southern wetlands I personally was a Yankee "out of water," so to speak, though being *in* the water was the rub. When photo hunting off-trail in wetland woods I was a bit freaked out about cottonmouth moccasins, owing not to real encounters but to locals regaling me with stories of close calls with these big and frightfully aggressive reptiles. I first wore high rubber boots and eventually adapted by sticking to trails when near swamps or rivers. I kept a vigilant eye out for reptiles—some friendly looking and some not so much—which did occasionally materialize.

Memorable and more carefree southern attractions include Georgia's Cumberland Island with its magnificent oaks; I'd go back tomorrow if I could. Florida's state park system is nationally renowned with paths through "hammocks" of high ground surrounded by sogginess. At upland terrain in Georgia and Alabama, tempting trails rival others of note that lie farther north along the East's topographic backbone.

In winter, the southern woods remain an indisputable attraction for wandering on foot. While the rest of the country is locked in a deep freeze, shoveling snow, or chipping at frozen rain, southern hiking is delectably springlike. Full-on springtime also appeals, but a lot of bugs get busy hatching then. Summer's a humid squelcher. Storm-driven rains from June to November astonish in their ability to penetrate and soak, and now, in the age of global warming, the hurricane season's getting worse—fully frightening as never before. Late autumn is worth the wait, with an amenable sweetness all its own in America's lowcountry forests.

Congaree National Park

LOCATION
southeast of Columbia

LENGTH
2 miles on boardwalks, plus more

DIFFICULTY
easy to moderate

TREE SPECIES
baldcypresses, water tupelos, loblolly pines, longleaf pines, sweetgums, 15 species of oaks

HIGHLIGHTS
baldcypresses in bottomland forest, tall hardwoods

PREVIOUS SPREAD: Springtime's warmth brings out the fan-compound leaves of a Fraser magnolia in Mississippi's Leaf Wilderness Area. A loblolly pine, eastern white oak, and overcup oak fill the background.

Totem trees of the Deep South, baldcypresses are the big attraction here. At home in wetlands along the Coastal Plain from Virginia to Texas, these deciduous conifers also populate lowlands of the Mississippi Valley up to Indiana. Baldcypresses are related to the redwoods of California and reflect the same gravitas. Though heavily cut for lumber, shingles, and even garden mulch, some of the finest remaining groves have been protected.

If the Deep South is the baldcypress nation of America—and it is—then Congaree is the capital city. This largest bloc of bottomland hardwood forest in the United States evaded complete clear-cutting for years through the hydrologic gift of the Congaree River's frequent flooding. It overflows with turbid runoff into the woodlands 10 times a year on average, which is enough to make logging difficult.

But over the years timber companies became less particular, and the forest was facing chain saws in 1969. A grassroots campaign inspired by newspaper editor Harry Hampton in nearby Columbia a decade earlier led to designation of Congaree as a national natural landmark and then a national monument in 1976. The 27,000-acre forest with 81 tree species was upgraded to a national park in 2003.

Primarily floodplain, 11,000 acres of old growth constitute one of the largest expanses of ancient forest in the East, though some areas were logged between 1897 and 1917, and 3,000 acres were clearcut in the 1970s as a last-ditch liquidation in the throes of the park campaign.

Congaree remains home to the tallest trees of 15 species as measured by the Eastern Native Tree Society's Will Blozan with Jess and Doug Riddle. Champion trees include a 167-foot loblolly pine, 157-foot sweetgum, 154-foot cherrybark oak, 135-foot American elm, 133-foot swamp chestnut oak, 131-foot overcup oak, and 127-foot persimmon—all likely taller now. Champion trees of the largest size (a multifaceted metric of overall mass) total 27 species. Virtually all these trees require off-trail searching by foot or canoe into remote floodplain locations—not for the average hiker.

Check in at the visitor center, consider a suite of available trails, and set off for the baldcypress stroll of a lifetime. A spectacular stand rises from the main boardwalk not far away. I loved early morning, when the trees' giant shadows were already welcome relief from the southern sun, and I was not even tempted to stray from the path through saturated terrain.

Walk the Low and High Boardwalk Trails for the finest baldcypresses. The River Trail aims onward to the Congaree River, where anticlimactic shores are populated by smaller tupelos in thickets. The 2-mile Bluff Trail reveals recovering longleaf pines and upland species. The Oakridge Trail of 7 miles leads to large Virginia live oaks. To tour the wetland forest more directly, paddle the Cedar Creek Canoe Trail of 15 miles, with care to not get lost. It's flat out there, all about the same, and often cloudy without the sun directly visible for orientation in this humid latitude, so take a compass and remember which side of major reference points you're on. Trail markers can be under water at times or hidden.

Winter here brings moderate temperatures and fewer bugs, but I wear protective clothing and take repellant for no-see-ums and a host of six-legged kin in all seasons. Spring and fall have a lot more color, including red maples, in their spacious range that extends from mountaintops in Maine down to sea level in Florida. While you'll likely see none, cottonmouth moccasins are common, especially in summer, and can appear in piles of black on the paths. Copperheads and canebrake rattlesnakes also make this home; be alert and ready to give wide berth. Enjoy great birding, and keep a curious eye peeled for turtles and alligators in this land where cold-blooded creatures don't have to worry much about a deep freeze.

From Columbia, drive I-77 south and take exit 5 onto Route 48/Bluff Road southeast. At 20 miles south of Columbia, turn south at Congaree's sign, and start at the visitor center.

Awendaw Passage, Francis Marion National Forest

SOUTH CAROLINA

LOCATION
north of Charleston

LENGTH
8 miles out and back, with options

DIFFICULTY
easy

TREE SPECIES
water oaks, dwarf palmettos, loblolly pines

HIGHLIGHTS
large water oaks, wetlands

The dwarf palmetto sets the Coastal Plain forests of the Southeast apart. These diagnostic short trees of lowlands thrive along the Awendaw Creek reach of the Palmetto Trail.

Francis Marion National Forest is the East Coast's only national forest pressing against Atlantic shores. It borders Cape Romain National Wildlife Refuge for 30 seaside miles, and the Awendaw Passage winds through forests and wetlands at nearly zero elevation.

Awendaw shows the effects of rising salt water on forests at our coastal edges. Sea level here is rising nearly a quarter inch per year—more than the troubling average worldwide—and effects are aggravated by droughts that diminish freshwater flow toward the ocean. Oaks are among the first trees to succumb to the increasing salinity.

The trail runs up floodplains of Awendaw Creek (an estuary here), passing through loblolly and dwarf palmetto thickets while passing sprawling water oaks edging tidal flows where the charismatic trees' remaining time is short.

Located between the Intracoastal Waterway and Highway 17, the passage connects with the Swamp Fox Passage, which gains elevation as it continues northward through Francis Marion National Forest, 47 miles to Lake Moultrie, and joins the Palmetto Trail, now discontinuous but planned to cross South Carolina to the Appalachian crest, 500 miles altogether.

From Charleston, drive north on Highway 17 for 27 miles, cross the Awendaw Creek, pass Steed Creek Road on the left, and in 3 miles turn right at the Palmetto Trail sign.

Cumberland Island National Seashore

GEORGIA

LOCATION
north of Jacksonville, Florida

LENGTH
1 to 5 miles

DIFFICULTY
easy

TREE SPECIES
Virginia live oaks, dwarf palmettos

HIGHLIGHTS
oaks, seaside forest

The weighty Virginia live oaks of Cumberland Island rank as one of the most magnificent tree species of the Southeast, with contorted limbs taking indirect but impressive routes toward the sun. With a thick understory of palmettos, these are signature stalwarts of the coastal forest, thriving here behind a barrier dune at Stafford Beach.

This designated national seashore is appealing in many ways but exceptional for its enormous oaks growing on stabilized dunes and amid thickets of vines, palmettos, and junglelike undergrowth.

Cumberland is known for expansive sandy beaches—spared a lineup of luxury hotels when acquired as parkland by the federal government. One of the most pristine Atlantic coastlines, this unit of the national park system draws visitors who hike, bike, camp, beach walk, and tour post–Civil War mansions built before the island became a public reserve in 1972.

For the full experience, I recommend camping on the island; reserve a site from the Park Service in advance. Sea Camp—at the southern end near the ferry dock—is home to aged maritime oaks. Also see Stafford Beach 3 miles north, and stroll the dune-edge trail farther for additional oaks.

The island's 50 miles of trails include access to a 9,800-acre wilderness at the north end. The Nightingale Trail traverses maritime oaks and palmettos. Bike on the Main Park Road. The Parallel Trail runs the same distance beneath serial umbrellas of overlapping oaks.

This ideal winter escape is also good in spring and fall if free of hurricanes, which are intensifying with global warming—a crisis also bringing sea-level rise and consequences for these cherished forests.

Reach the island by ferryboat, which launches twice each morning from the town of St. Marys at the Georgia-Florida border. From I-95, 3 miles north of the Florida line, take exit 3, drive Route 40 east 6 miles, turn right on St. Marys Street, and park in the ferryboat lot. Get tickets there, but reserve ahead of time. Walk-ins can buy unclaimed tickets, but don't count on them.

Tallulah Gorge State Park

GEORGIA

LOCATION
south of Clayton in northeast Georgia

LENGTH
3 miles round trip

DIFFICULTY
easy on the rim, strenuous beyond

TREE SPECIES
sweetgums, oaks, Virginia pines

HIGHLIGHTS
Appalachian gorge with southern tree species

Vivid colors of sweetgum and red maple commune on rock ledges in Tallulah Gorge. Red maples have one of the widest ranges of eastern trees, populating forests and wetlands from Canada to the tip of Florida and from Atlantic shores to Minnesota and Texas. Sweetgums are natives of the South, but have been planted widely for their beauty.

OPPOSITE: Tallulah Gorge cuts deeply into the southern terminus of the Appalachians. Near this meeting of mountains and Piedmont, the forest includes a mix of northern and southern trees. Virginia pines cling to cliff faces, and oaks of several species warm with autumn color in October.

This steep walk into one of the Appalachian Mountains' most notable gorges—unexpected by many this far south—winds down 1,000 feet through forests with southern trees such as sweetgum, sourwood, and silverbell. A chain of rapids and waterfalls makes the reputation of this 2,700-acre state park, but the forests are likewise exceptional.

Start at the visitor center and plan a hike to match your fitness. Stroll the rim or descend hundreds of steps to the bottom of the gorge and the thrilling footbridge suspended above Hurricane Falls. The Sliding Rock Trail, equivalent to a black-diamond ski slope, requires a permit.

Springtime is inviting here, and autumn is vivid with the complementary scarlet and orange of red maples and sweetgums.

From I-985 northeast of Atlanta, take Highway 23 north to Tallulah Gorge State Park, 11 miles before Clayton.

Nearby hikes tour southern Appalachian forests along the Chattooga River bordering Georgia and South Carolina. Trail walking along this famous whitewater river starts at Burrells Ford Bridge and heads downstream with pools for swimming. See the Chattahoochee National Forest map for more information.

Cloudland Canyon State Park

GEORGIA

LOCATION
southwest of Chattanooga,
Tennessee

LENGTH
2 to 6 miles

DIFFICULTY
strenuous

TREE SPECIES
tulip trees, oaks, hemlocks

HIGHLIGHTS
waterfalls and southern
Appalachian forest

A surprise to me in Georgia's northwest corner, this ruggedly scenic, forested canyon has been carved by Bear Creek and tributaries into Lookout Mountain—upraised on the west side of the Cumberland Plateau, which extends from Kentucky to here near the southern limit of the Appalachian Mountains.

Stroll the Overlook Trail to canyon views. But for the real deal, a 2-mile Waterfalls Trail descends 600 steps to Cherokee and Hemlock Falls. The West Rim Loop Trail of 5 miles includes additional views, and the Sitton's Gulch Trail passes 5 miles through some of the Appalachians' southernmost hemlock groves, whose remoteness has spared them the adelgid plague as of this writing, but probably not for long unless the trees are treated.

In this park with robust visitation from Chattanooga and nearby towns, spring and fall are best, on weekdays or at early and late hours. Trails are open in winter when mountain cold snaps can turn the waterfalls to ice, even at Georgia latitudes.

From Chattanooga, drive west on I-24 and exit south on Highway 59/406. At Trenton, turn east on Route 136. Continue 9.5 miles and then turn left into the park.

Hemlocks and rhododendrons tap spare soils of their rocky landscape along the Waterfalls Trail in Cloudland Canyon State Park.

OPPOSITE: Hemlock Falls and a towering tulip tree compete for vertical attention along the Waterfalls Trail in Cloudland Canyon State Park.

Sipsey Wilderness, Bankhead National Forest

ALABAMA

LOCATION
northwest of Birmingham

LENGTH
1 to 5 miles

DIFFICULTY
easy to moderate

TREE SPECIES
beeches, oaks, sweet birches, tulip trees

HIGHLIGHTS
beech forest, Sipsey Fork streamside

A Deep South outpost in the Appalachians, the Sipsey Wilderness of 25,770 acres features 45 miles of trails through hills, stream corridors beneath sandstone cliffs 100 feet high, and waterfalls of Bankhead National Forest. Sipsey Fork (of the Black Warrior River) and nine small tributaries are the only designated national wild and scenic rivers in Alabama.

The Sipsey River Trail, 5 miles out and back, starts along the small stream and tours a rich mix of tree species. Nearly all was logged before wilderness designation, but a few old-growth enclaves survived.

From Birmingham, drive west on I-22 to Jasper, jog north around town to Route 195, and continue north to Double Springs. Turn right on Route 33, left on CR 60/Cranal Road, and continue to the bridge and trailhead.

Sipsey Wilderness, located where the Appalachian Mountains taper down toward the Gulf of Mexico's Coastal Plain, is Alabama's finest wilderness. Beech trees had evolutionary roots in the Deep South before they began their progression northward in the aftermath of the continental glaciers.

Highlands Hammock State Park

FLORIDA

LOCATION
northeast of Fort Myers

LENGTH
1 to 3 miles

DIFFICULTY
easy

TREE SPECIES
Virginia oaks, baldcypresses,
longleaf pines, pignut hickories,
sabal palms

HIGHLIGHTS
hammock ecosystem, big oaks,
recovering longleaf pines

The burled base of a 1,000-year-old
Virginia live oak stands at Highlands
Hammock State Park. One of many
excellent parks in the subtropical state,
this one combines upraised "hammocks"
of drier ground with wetlands typical of
Florida's Coastal Plain.

OPPOSITE: Each step on the trails
of Highlands Hammock State Park
reveals a spicy mix of trees and
junglelike understory. Here, pignut
hickory leaves catch morning light on
the left, sabal palms rise on the right,
and other plants fill every cranny in
the subtropical ecosystem.

Many of Florida's 175 state parks offer trails among subtropical trees unique in America. Highlands Hammock is just one, but an excellent choice for paths, tree diversity, and near-tropical conditions in southcentral Florida. State park literature credits this 9,000-acre reserve with more rare and endemic species than any other location statewide. Cougars, black bears, and alligators make home here, and, in contrast to Florida's domineering pop-culture glitz, Highlands Hammock earns the state park department's slogan, "the real Florida."

From the main parking lot, set off on any one of the trails featuring hammock ecosystems—upraised domes of topography formed by limestone and dunes surrounded by lower wetlands, all yielding remarkably varied flora. Fires ignited by frequent tumultuous thunderstorms building in afternoons and starkly illuminating the black of night are also integral to the age-old ecological process. Boardwalks and paths include the half-mile Cypress Swamp Trail and the 3-mile Wild Orange and Hickory Loop.

Virginia live oaks rooted in upland terrain grow large and bulky here. The park is also home to longleaf pines, once covering millions of acres of southern land with fat, arrow-straight trunks, but virtually eradicated for timber and plantations.

Though the pines at this park—and most restoration sites—are not strikingly large, a new forest is underway, and each year the longleafs inch toward three-foot diameters that future generations of visitors will hopefully see.

From Fort Myers, drive northeast on Highway 80, merge north on Highway 27, and continue north from Sebring to the park road on the left.

A few of my other favorite Florida forest reserves are Alexander Springs of Ocala National Forest, in the northcentral part of the state, which has sabal palms, palmettos, and pignut hickories around its broad crystalline spring; Myakka River State Park, which has a canopy tower offering a unique bird's-eye view down to a palm thicket; and Osceola National Forest in northern Florida, which showcases baldcypresses flooded in swamp water, best seen from a canoe.

Longleaf pines once blanketed the South as a seemingly endless forest of tall columns. Fire-adapted in a geography subject to epidemic thunderstorms and lightning strikes, the pines supported wildlife including endangered red-cockaded woodpeckers. The woodpeckers require longleafs for their oozing sap, which protects the birds' cavity nests and eggs from predatory tree-climbing snakes. Park managers at Highlands Hammock State Park and other southern sites have launched restoration efforts to bring the longleafs back where they can be managed with frequent controlled fires, which the pines require.

MIDWEST

Most of the Midwest was once a seamless continuation of eastern forests stretching toward the Great Plains except for clearings by fire, wind, and flood. Though a bit of a stretch, a cute cliché says a squirrel could scamper from the Atlantic to the Great Plains without leaving the canopy (it would have to swim the Mississippi River, but squirrels—unequivocally the masters of the treetops—somehow *do* know how to swim!). Now much of the region is planted in soybeans and corn for cattle, chickens, and pigs, and the squirrels are gone.

However, central hardwoods once grew better than corn does, with a lot more biomass, and isolated groves can still be found, ever more precious for their scarcity. Here we have bur oaks instead of the chestnut oaks found eastward, blue ashes instead of white ashes, and black walnuts, butternuts, hickories, and cottonwoods.

A vast midwestern forest remains in the northern tier of Michigan, Wisconsin, and Minnesota. Logging eliminated white pines that had crowned this territory, which is now a mix of alders in wetlands, white pines in recovering stands, and a lot of New England's other tree species—as if Vermont were dragged to midcontinent, flattening it in the process.

Throughout most of the Midwest, major trails are few, but local groves have luring pathways, town parks offer woodland strolls, and trails can be found in eight national forests across the northern tier, with another three southward in the Ozark region of regrowing oaks and hickories. Most of this public land was acquired during the Great Depression, and it remains a patchwork of national forest and private inholdings.

In the north, harsh winters are open to savvy skiers or snowshoers. Springtime is a tonic, but the bugs can be maddening from warm-up through summer; be prepared, including taking precautions against ticks. Northern-tier hiking is best in autumn, when warm colors of maples, birches, aspens, cottonwoods, and oaks are as captivating as almost anywhere else in the country.

Beaver Creek State Park

OHIO

LOCATION
south of Youngstown

LENGTH
1 to 3 miles

DIFFICULTY
easy

TREE SPECIES
sycamores, hemlocks, oaks, maples

HIGHLIGHTS
sycamores along the creek

PREVIOUS SPREAD: Aged yellow birches and hemlocks highlight the Guido Rahr Sr. Tenderfoot Forest Reserve in Wisconsin.

In November autumn's brightness fades, but colors linger along Little Beaver Creek's Middle Fork. Sycamores with their mottled bark grow at the water's edge, where they tolerate flooding for weeks at a time. Hemlocks grip steep slopes in the Appalachian's westernmost foothills.

This stream-centric state park offers a fine example of a woods reclaimed after two centuries of farming and where forest succession again plays out. The preserve lies at the interface of foothills ramping eastward up to the Appalachian Plateau and fading westward to midcontinent farms and fields. The centerpiece is actually the Middle Fork of Little Beaver Creek (not Beaver Creek, and neither should be confused with the Beaver River, just eastward).

Unblocked by steep or high topography, the continental glaciers crept down surprisingly far from the north, then retreated, leaving a legacy of cold-climate plant life, including hemlocks and birches.

Where the main road bridges the creek, park and walk the left-shore trail facing downstream, where fat sycamores grace riparian thickets. Other paths connect eastward to ridge routes, where hemlocks still thrive and recovering hardwoods invest girth every year.

For this low-key, out-of-the-way park, start at East Liverpool on the Pennsylvania boundary and drive north on Highway 30/11. Bear right on Route 7 north, turn right on Birch Road, jog west, and then resume north on Bell School Road and Route 929 to the park entrance. Or aim for the park south of the village of Clarkson.

Goll Woods State Nature Preserve

This is among the finest of the rare preserved groves of old trees in the 10-state Corn Belt. An easy loop tours the 321-acre plot of hardwoods, some four feet across and rooted in a remnant of the fertile Black Swamp that typified postglacial flats south of the Great Lakes before farmers gridded tile drainage and bulldozed ditches throughout. This is the most intact forest in northwestern Ohio, and a registered national natural landmark.

Early spring and autumn are good. Expect mosquitoes in late spring and summer.

On I-80/Ohio Turnpike, drive east from Indiana 26 miles to exit 25. Take Highway 66 south, and in 3.4 miles turn right on F Road, then left on Route 26 to the entrance.

LOCATION
east of the Indiana border, northwest of Archbold

LENGTH
1 mile

DIFFICULTY
easy

TREE SPECIES
white oaks, bur oaks, chinquapin oaks, eastern cottonwoods, tulip trees, silver and red maples, hickories

HIGHLIGHTS
some of the largest trees in Ohio

Goll Woods State Nature Preserve is a rare old-growth tract that escaped the wholesale mowing of midwestern forests. Here, an aged eastern cottonwood stands in the foreground, tulip trees with similar bark rise to its right, a red oak with its darkly shaded trunk holds the center, and a mature beech shines silvery in the background.

Hemmer Woods Nature Preserve

INDIANA

LOCATION
northeast of Evansville

LENGTH
0.5 miles

DIFFICULTY
easy

TREE SPECIES
oaks, mockernut hickories,
shagbark hickories

HIGHLIGHTS
large midwestern hardwoods

Hemmer Woods Nature Preserve is a 73-acre respite of mature hardwoods amid a sea of farms and strip mines in southern Indiana. A loop trail crosses upland and lowland tree zones with a mix of black, white, and red oaks; white ashes (as long as the emerald ash borer doesn't infect them); pignut, mockernut, and shagbark hickories; sassafras, tulip trees, river birches, sycamores, and black cherries; sugar maples from the north; and some lowland or southern species, including sweetgums.

Hemmer Woods is a reminder of the richly diverse forest that once blanketed southern Indiana and much of the Midwest. Unfortunately, a windstorm in 2012 leveled half the trees in portions of the preserve, reminding us that small remnant groves are vulnerable to wind damage after surrounding trees have been removed. Larger preserves are needed, if only to plant new perimeter forests of the future as a means to protect our precious forests of the past.

From I-64, take exit 29 at Elberfeld, go north on Route 57 past Route 68, and take exit 57 at Buckskin onto CR 900S. Go east 2.5 miles to the fourth intersection, and on CR 1050E go north half a mile to the park entrance on the right.

Hemmer Woods Nature Preserve offers a glimpse of the hardwoods estate that once covered much of the Midwest—now the Corn Belt. Here, on a foggy morning in late autumn, sugar maples cling to yellow leaves, oaks of several species share their space, and hickories typify the eastern deciduous forest in its western reaches.

Gebhard Woods State Park

ILLINOIS

This park is only 30 acres, but I feature it here for its canopy of black walnut trees with diagnostically compound, long-pointed leaves. Rich crops of golf ball–size nuts condense nutritious food stores for wildlife, while thick layers of fallen leaves shield the soil from erosion beneath the canopy. Other hardwoods seen here were once typical across the heart of the Midwest: oaks, ashes, maples, sycamores, hawthorns, and eastern cottonwoods.

Marketed for their finely grained, dark lumber, walnut trees garner top prices as hardwoods. Most are now grown in plantations to be cut and crafted into furniture. Mature native groves—even small ones like this one—have become rare.

Bordered on the south by the historic Illinois and Michigan Canal, and beyond that by the broad Illinois River, the park connects with a footbridge to the canal's biking and walking trail of 61 miles from west of Chicago at Lemont to La Salle.

On I-80, drive west from Chicago 50 miles. At exit 112/Morris, go south on Route 47/Division Street, turn right on Jefferson Street (which becomes Fremont Avenue), and then turn left into the park.

LOCATION
southwest of Chicago, west of Morris

LENGTH
0.5 miles

DIFFICULTY
easy

TREE SPECIES
black walnuts, oaks, maples

HIGHLIGHTS
large black walnut trees

Black walnut trees, with their nutrient-packed nuts, are a nearly forgotten keystone species of eastern and midwestern forests. Here, at Gebhard Woods State Park southwest of Chicago, the walnuts' enveloping crowns with their sharply compound leaves can still be seen.

Cathedral Pines Campground, Huron-Manistee National Forest

MICHIGAN

LOCATION
east of Grayling

LENGTH
0.5 miles out and back

DIFFICULTY
easy

TREE SPECIES
white pines

HIGHLIGHTS
tall white pines, rare old growth

This small, lightly visited site is undeveloped and principally used as a canoe-in campsite along the Au Sable River between Comins Flats, east of Mio, and McKinley Bridge in Huron-Manistee National Forest—a crowd-free escape to some big pines. The evergreens tower overhead as they once did from horizon to horizon in the upper Midwest before the logging of the late 1800s.

On I-75, drive to the northern reaches of Michigan's Lower Peninsula. At Grayling/exit 254, take Route 72 east, pass through Mio, and go 6 miles to the obscure dirt road FR 4350. Turn left, drive to the end, and walk a quarter mile to the Au Sable River. Or paddle there from a canoe access off McKinley Road to the northwest, which is how I found this intimate grove.

Scarce and scattered, a few other old-growth stands in Michigan escaped the saw. Consider Hartwick Pines State Park northeast of Grayling, Newton Woods at the Fred Russ Forest Experimental Station in southwestern Michigan, and Sylvania Wilderness of Ottawa National Forest on the western Upper Peninsula.

The Cathedral Pines rise over the Au Sable River. Reached by canoe for this photo, but also by a quarter-mile walk from a dirt road, the grove glows in sunrise upstream from McKinley Bridge.

Grand Island

MICHIGAN

LOCATION
Upper Peninsula near
Munising

LENGTH
20-mile bike trail loop

DIFFICULTY
easy, but a full day of biking

TREE SPECIES
red, white, and jack pines,
sugar and red maples, white
spruces, paper birches

HIGHLIGHTS
forested island in
Lake Superior

Grand Island is a retreat visited with a half-mile ferryboat ride from Michigan's Upper Peninsula and a 20-mile loop trail. This former private hunting reserve was acquired by the Forest Service as a national recreation area in 1990.

Walk your mountain bike onto the ferryboat and then pedal counterclockwise up the island's west shore and back down the center or east side. The trail is also good for easy walking and backpacking. Forested and scenic, especially at its watery west and north aspects, the loop trail features red pines, white pines, mixed hardwoods, and magnificent beech trees that unfortunately have succumbed to the beech bark disease that has migrated from the blight's source in Nova Scotia to here at the western limit of the stately tree's range. Fat-tired mountain bikes are needed on the smooth but intermittently sandy trails. Ferries run hourly in summer; the cost was $20 in 2020.

On Highway 28 across the Upper Peninsula, drive west from Munising and watch for Grand Island's sign on the right. Turn right on Grand Island Landing Road and follow it to the ferry.

White pines thrive on Grand Island above steep banks that drop precipitously into the largest of the Great Lakes.

Porcupine Mountains Wilderness State Park

MICHIGAN

LOCATION
Upper Peninsula, west side at Lake Superior

LENGTH
1 mile and more out and back, or loops

DIFFICULTY
easy to strenuous

TREE SPECIES
sugar maples, hemlocks, white pines

HIGHLIGHTS
hemlocks, northern hardwoods

With forests remarkably similar to those of New England, this 60,000-acre state park is one of the largest wilderness areas in the Midwest and among the largest nationwide under state jurisdiction. Half is old growth, though much of that is stunted or subject to fire, wind, and wetlands. This is the only "mountain range" in the upper Midwest.

Some of the westernmost eastern hemlocks occupy a stronghold here, as the onslaught of woolly adelgid may take time to reach this far from its death grip on the hemlocks of the East, and the exotic insect is curtailed by acutely cold winters; untreated trees might survive here longer than elsewhere south of Canada. White pines, tulip trees, sugar maples, paper birches, and basswoods do well in the varied microclimate near Lake Superior.

With access off Route 107 in the park's northeast quadrant, trails finger 90 miles through the Porcupines, visit beaches, traverse mixed forests in various stages of succession following the Wisconsin Ice Age, and climb to summits, including 1,500-foot Porcupine Mountain and similar LaFayette Peak. The Carp River basin has old hemlocks and sugar maples.

From Highway 28 on the Upper Peninsula, turn north on Route 64, go to Silver City, and turn left on Route 107.

The Porcupine Mountains are the Midwest's closest claim to a mountain range, topping out at 1,952 feet and dropping to Lake Superior. Sugar maples dominate here in the Carp River basin.

Guido Rahr Sr. Tenderfoot Forest Reserve

The Guido Rahr Sr. Tenderfoot Reserve of The Nature Conservancy is located at Wisconsin's remote border with Michigan's Upper Peninsula. It can only be reached with a 3-mile, one-way paddle from a dock on adjacent Palmer Lake.

The trail winds among aged hemlocks, 400-year-old white pines, and large yellow birches while spruces and balsam firs shade the shore. Five hundred acres constitute one of the Midwest's largest old-growth sites.

Open to the public, this reserve can be reached by boat from ice-out in May to October. Prepare for bugs in summer or a sharp chill in shoulder seasons. September is ideal.

Bear with me here for this hidden site: in northeastern Wisconsin, at Minocqua, go north on Highway 51. Turn right on Route M, stay on it past Boulder Junction and Wildcat Lake's south shore, and then turn right on Route B. After 9 miles, angle sharp left onto Palmer Lake Road and continue 2 miles to the dock. Take your canoe or kayak off the car (no boats are available there) and paddle to the northwest corner of Palmer Lake, then into the broad outlet of the Ontonagon River. Paddle down the slow-moving stream 1 mile (it's easy to return back upriver; just remember the route), enter the sizable Tenderfoot Lake, paddle toward the opposite shore and around an island to the lake's northwest side, and watch for the inconspicuous landing and loop trail.

In this state where only 0.3 percent of original old growth remains, consider also Cathedral Pines State Natural Area in Chequamegon-Nicolet National Forest near Lakewood, where a short trail tours 200- to 400-year-old white pines, red pines, and hemlocks.

WISCONSIN

LOCATION
northern Wisconsin, north of Woodruff

LENGTH
2-mile loop, with access by canoe

DIFFICULTY
easy, but paddling is necessary

TREE SPECIES
hemlocks, white pines, northern hardwoods

HIGHLIGHTS
hemlocks, large yellow birches, northern conifers

The Guido Rahr Sr. Tenderfoot Forest Reserve is accessible only by paddling across Palmer Lake and down the Ontonagon River, shown here with hemlocks on the right and balsam firs—more typical of the Far North—on the left.

Nerstrand Big Woods State Park

MINNESOTA

LOCATION
south of Minneapolis and
Northfield

LENGTH
1-mile loop

DIFFICULTY
easy

TREE SPECIES
sugar maples, basswoods,
green ashes, ironwoods

HIGHLIGHTS
old hardwoods

A loop trail wanders across this gentle landscape covered by tall deciduous trees—the largest remnant of what was once the "Big Woods" blanketing central Minnesota before farmers arrived. The 2,900-acre park is best visited in May with wildflowers, and in fall with brilliant colors. Prep for bugs in late spring and summer.

From Minneapolis, drive south on I-35 to exit 69 and go east on Highway 19 to Northfield. In the town's center, turn right, head south on Route 246, continue 11 miles to a four-way stop, and turn right on Route 29 to the park.

Other old forests in Minnesota can be found at George Crosby Manitou State Park, which includes several hundred acres of hardwoods on the northwest shore of Lake Superior. Itasca Wilderness Sanctuary, within Itasca State Park at the headwaters of the Mississippi, has a lot of small trees, but also 4,000 acres of old pines and 120 acres of old hardwoods. The North Country National Scenic Trail crosses the upper-tier states from New York to North Dakota, and a wild Minnesota section crosses the Boundary Waters Canoe Area Wilderness with acreage not logged for decades, though fires have burned, wind takes a toll, and wetlands restrict tree size. In this remote wilderness, early autumn is best, and paddling's the way to go if you have a canoe.

Nerstrand Big Woods State Park is named for the forest that once unified much of eastern Minnesota—now covered with corn. This park secures a remnant of magnificent hardwoods including sugar maples, basswoods, oaks, and beeches.

Temperance River and Cascade River State Parks

MINNESOTA

LOCATION
North Shore of Lake Superior

LENGTH
1 to 5 miles or more, out and back or loops

DIFFICULTY
easy to moderate

TREE SPECIES
northern white cedars, paper birches, eastern white pines, balsam firs

HIGHLIGHTS
aged cedars, clusters of paper birches, waterfalls, Lake Superior

Paper birches are emblematic of the northern states, but they are tragically being decimated by the bronze birch borer and a warming climate, especially on south-facing slopes. Here, at Temperance River State Park, they join with white spruces and dwarf honeysuckles in the boreal forest spanning Canada—the largest woodland type in total mass across the continent.

OPPOSITE: A white pine rises above the northern forest at Cascade River State Park. The great pines once characterized the northern forest through New England and the upper Midwest. Comprehensively logged in the late 1800s, they are now recovering across much of their range.

These two state parks offer a sampling of the boreal and northern hardwood forests of Lake Superior's North Shore—spectacular enough to be a national park, though it's not. Both state preserves feature birches, a suite of conifers, waterfalls, and gorges.

Temperance River State Park lies 81 miles northeast of Duluth and just past Schroeder. Trails line both riverbanks. Park along Highway 61 or reach trailheads between campground sites 14 and 25. Fees may be charged.

Cascade River State Park is 101 miles from Duluth and south of Grand Marais. Park at the mouth of the river along Highway 61. The wooded Cascade River Trail leads to five waterfalls.

Autumn is dazzling here when birches turn yellow. Ski trails open later at Cascade. Spring is welcome with its long-awaited thaw, and summer is beautiful with lake breezes that keep the bugs down.

Other state parks also appeal along the lake's North Shore, and the Superior Hiking Trail passes through both Temperance River and Cascade River State Parks on its 300-mile route from the Minnesota-Wisconsin line to Canada, perched on ridgelines overlooking America's largest lake.

Mount Theodore Roosevelt, Black Hills National Forest

LOCATION
**Black Hills National Forest
southeast of Spearfish**

LENGTH
1-mile out and back

DIFFICULTY
easy

PRIMARY TREES
ponderosa pines, aspens

HIGHLIGHTS
Rocky Mountain—type forest

Named for their green pines, whose darkness is overstated but nonetheless blackish compared to the pale prairie surrounding them, the Black Hills loom high enough above the Great Plains to catch the snow and rain that nourish ponderosa pines and quaking aspens, much like in the Rocky Mountains, whose main escarpment awaits a full 120 miles farther west. For anyone crossing the Great Plains and impatient for a conifer forest, this short jog off I-90 to Black Hills National Forest is the ticket.

The trail to a tower atop Mount Theodore Roosevelt, 5,676 feet above sea level, offers a view of this arboreal island rising from the sea of prairie. Sunrise and sunset glow beautifully through summer's clear skies.

On I-90, drive west from Sturgis, take exit 17 and Highway 85 south 7 miles, and then turn right on FR 133 (1 mile short of the 85-14A intersection) to the parking lot. Hike through pines and aspens to a fire tower open to tourists.

At Mount Theodore Roosevelt, daybreak silhouettes ponderosa pines along the path to the summit.

OPPOSITE: Far west across the Great Plains, the Black Hills of South Dakota rise as an outlier of the Rocky Mountains surrounded by short-grass prairie. The uplifted terrain collects rain and snow to grow aspens and ponderosa pines like those seen farther west.

ROCKY MOUNTAINS
AND WESTERN DRYLANDS

The Rocky Mountains stretch from Canada to New Mexico with their own cast of woodlands entirely different from any in the East or at the Pacific coast. Just west of the Rockies, the Great Basin includes 200 relatively small isolated ranges across Nevada and adjacent states with scattered high forests and life-supporting ribbons of streamside trees.

Mountains of the interior West have not one timberline but two: most trees cannot grow below a certain elevation because of insufficient rain or snowfall, and they cannot grow above the level where snow, wind, cold, and bedrock prevent survival.

Within high mountain valleys narrowleaf cottonwoods crowd riverfronts, while lower valleys have black cottonwoods—signature trees of the interior West. Downstream and fingering into the plains and deserts, Fremont cottonwoods with heart-shaped leaves continue the *Populus* niche, and in northern latitudes similar balsam poplars excel. These broadleaf cousins share a sweet scent signifying springtime and also ecological importance as keystone species on which varied wildlife depend. Along with eastern cottonwoods, these five are among 11 very large broadleaf trees in America (others are sycamores, valley oaks, Virginia live oaks, tulip trees, bigleaf maples, and American elms).

Related to cottonwoods, but smaller in the poplar family, quaking aspens brighten sunny slopes, resprout vigorously after fires, and emblematize the Rockies' midelevations, though these cosmopolitan trees also claim the largest arboreal range in North America: from the Bering Sea to Labrador, and from near-Arctic to mid-Mexico. By one biological metric, aspens are the oldest and largest tree: whole assemblages are cloned to the same root-mass and might be considered one giant organism, though above ground they clearly appear as individual trees and can survive as such. Clonal families can be identified in autumn by distinctive colors—orange here, yellow there. At Fishlake National Forest in Utah, one of these common root sources covers 106 acres with 47,000 trees.

Also thriving in the wake of flames, lodgepole pines thicken in monocultures of the Rockies from medium-high elevations down to terrain with only 14 inches of precipitation per year. Engelmann spruces dominate above. Higher still, whitebark and limber pines brave winter storms and shed pine nuts serving jays, Clark's nutcrackers, and bears. Both these pine species are being decimated by white-pine blister rust, a fungal disease from Europe affecting the entire family of five-needled pines—tall eastern whites and western whites included.

In high ranges of the Great Basin, bristlecone pines survive for an incredible 4,000 years in habitat that's harsh, cold, and spare, but thereby protected from rot, insects, and fire.

Picturesque at timberline, wind-sculpted krummholz are weatherdwarfed versions of mountain hemlocks, spruces, and firs shaped by continental winds to become living sculptures at the edges of snowbanks, rock gardens, and alpine meadows, all evoking the weather-worn essence of the West's high mountains.

In drylands at lower elevations, the woods are lean, but saguaro cacti symbolize the Sonoran Desert, paloverde harbor chlorophyll in their stems because larger leaves would suffer desiccating moisture loss, and Arizona's own species of sycamore shades streambanks.

With much of the terrain above 6,000 feet being publicly owned as national forests, the Rockies are a land of trails. Long-distance routes include the Continental Divide Trail of 2,624 miles and the Colorado Trail of 486 miles. Unlike the Appalachians, where forests tend to be the main attraction even on paths gripping ridgelines, the big draw here are the mountains with their views above timberline, cascading rivers, and lakes tucked like blue lenses into cirque basins carved earlier by glaciers. Trees in the Rockies' relatively spare surroundings don't grow like they do in the East or at the West Coast, and they are also prone to superheated stand-replacing fires, so most don't live long enough to become extremely old or large, except for the timberline masters of adversity. At low elevations, where trees can bulk to stately sizes, cutting during the mining and logging eras has left little of a rich heritage standing, yet some notable groves or individuals remain.

Lingering snow determines the season for hiking in the Rockies. Many areas don't open for traditional trekking until midsummer, and mosquitoes can thicken until soggy pockets of moisture evaporate, leaving an accessible mountain wonderland. Though nights are cold, sunny days of autumn are exquisite when cottonwoods, willows, and aspens brighten to yellow and gold.

Ross Creek Cedars Scenic Area

MONTANA

Western redcedars in the Ross Creek Cedars Scenic Area of northern Montana are the finest old-growth grove of large trees that I know of within the interior West. Methuselahs here live up to 1,000 years or more and reach 175 feet in height, with diameters up to 12 feet—the closest thing to redwoods in the Rockies. Not just scattered individuals, they crowd as a dense community on this 100-acre reserve. Of course, this is just postage-stamp size considering what once was. The scenic area was established in 1960, before the Wilderness Act, when few groves of any kind were protected from cutting.

Visit here spring through fall. From Troy—a logging town west of Libby near the Idaho border—drive east on Highway 2 for 3 miles, turn south on Route 56, and go 18 miles. At the end of Bull Lake, go right on Ross Creek Cedars Road for 4 miles.

Along this line, the Bernard DeVoto Memorial Grove—which has ancient western redcedars with six-foot-diameter trees—straddles Highway 12 west from the Idaho-Montana line.

LOCATION
south of Troy

LENGTH
1-mile loop

DIFFICULTY
easy

TREE SPECIES
western redcedars

HIGHLIGHTS
ancient forest, some of the largest trees in the Rockies

PREVIOUS SPREAD: In early summer, cream-colored buckwheat and violet fleabane daisies bloom at the edge of an aspen grove in Colorado's Routt National Forest. Scarlet gilia show their color, and fireweed spikes with purple in the background.

Perhaps the most extraordinary grove of ancient large trees in the Rocky Mountain region, the Ross Creek cedars have stood for 1,000 years along a small stream in northern Montana. The loop trail through this grove is the Rockies' version of the Pacific coast's redwoods.

Stillwater River

MONTANA

LOCATION
southwest of Columbus

LENGTH
1 mile or more out and back

DIFFICULTY
easy to strenuous

TREE SPECIES
Douglas firs, lodgepole pines,
Engelmann spruces, black
cottonwoods

HIGHLIGHTS
Rocky Mountain conifers
along a river

Trees along the Stillwater River are typical of mid-elevation forests in the central or northern Rockies. Douglas firs, lodgepole pines, and Engelmann spruces green this scenic canyon bottom from the end of Nye Road and southward into the heart of the Absaroka-Beartooth Wilderness, which extends up to Yellowstone National Park. Here, in prime grizzly bear country, make noise when in brush or at blind bends in the trail, keep a spotless camp, and carry food in bear canisters. I've hiked alone in grizzly country a lot, but going in a small group is far better to avoid bear problems and would always be my first choice.

Walk upstream any distance. The first mile passes through a gorge with Rocky Mountain forest, then through interludes of meadows and avalanche chutes riddling steep canyonsides. Day hikers can go 3 miles to Sioux Charley Lake. Beyond lie many miles for wilderness backpacking that link to other trails in the Absaroka Mountains and Beartooth Plateau. Lower mileage here can be done in late spring and early summer, when higher country of the Rockies remains snowbound.

From I-90 exit 408 at Columbus, go south on Route 78 for 27 miles to Absarokee. In another 3 miles, turn right on Nye Road and continue on it 29 miles to the end.

The Stillwater River Trail enters a canyon forested with Douglas firs here in the foreground.

St. Joe River

LOCATION
east of Saint Maries

LENGTH
1 mile or more out and back;
21 miles point to point

DIFFICULTY
moderate to strenuous

TREE SPECIES
subalpine firs, black
cottonwoods, Engelmann
spruces

HIGHLIGHTS
northern Rocky Mountain
forest, wild wooded canyon

Idaho is mostly forested within its Rocky Mountain province, and northern Idaho is wetter than latitudes to the south, so its forests resemble those of the interior Pacific Northwest. Still, trees tend not to get extremely large owing to logging and fires where summers are dry, thunderstorms are frequent, and winds are intense. The legendary 1910 Big Burn consumed 3 million acres, including the St. Joe River basin. Joe Halm and his crew found refuge at a gravel bar where headwaters of the St. Joe barely saved their lives—a story told by Timothy Egan in *The Big Burn*. In recent years, fires have been increasingly altering the landscape throughout the Rocky Mountains.

The trail up the St. Joe tours northern Rocky Mountain forests that have been regrowing since the Big Burn more than a century ago. Subalpine firs reach uncommon girth in habitat that's unusually low and moist for such a highcountry species. Western redcedars steal the arboreal show on floodplains as they do closer to the Pacific. Lodgepole pines blanket slopes veering to 6,000 feet, as do Engelmann spruces here at the heart of their range, though they remain common southward through the Rockies and grow larger in the Cascade Mountains of Washington and British Columbia.

Native cutthroat and bull trout thrive in the St. Joe, dependent on unlogged headwater forests for clean, shaded runoff. Moose, wolves, grizzly bears, wolverines, and mountain lions still roam.

From Spruce Tree Campground, the trail probes upstream 21 wild miles to where the road touches down again at Heller Creek Campground, though the gravel byway may be snowed in through June. Horseback riders heavily use the St. Joe Trail, which is dusty in late summer.

From Route 3 at Saint Maries, drive east on FR 50 and go 87 paved miles to Spruce Tree Campground and the trailhead. If approaching from the north or east, reach the St. Joe by exiting I-90 at St. Regis, Montana. Drive southward 28 miles on gravel FR 282, top Gold Summit, and descend paved FR 50 to the St. Joe road 12 miles west of Spruce Tree.

The St. Joe River flows from wild headwaters, where Engelmann spruces and cottonwoods shade the water and protect the rare native bull trout and westslope cutthroat trout that need chilled flows and long, undammed river mileage, which have become rare across the West.

Wild Basin Trail, Rocky Mountain National Park

COLORADO

LOCATION
southwest of Estes Park

LENGTH
6 miles out and back to Ouzel Falls and longer

DIFFICULTY
moderate

TREE SPECIES
lodgepole pines, Engelmann spruces

HIGHLIGHTS
Rocky Mountain conifer forest

The Wild Basin Trail is an excellent hike for immersion in a typical forest of the Colorado Rockies. Here, along North Saint Vrain Creek, Engelmann spruces, white firs, and lodgepole pines green the scene as Eric Krell and Ann Vileisis stride toward alpine terrain. Expect summer showers—just clearing here—and thunderstorms at high elevations in the afternoons.

OPPOSITE: A savvy little lodgepole pine grips rocks with roots that probe deep into cracks along North Saint Vrain Creek, while an aspen on the right flutters in the breeze and Engelmann spruces crowd in deeper soils.

In a national park famous for rigorous climbs and soaring views above timberline, this lower-terrain hike along North Saint Vrain Creek features typical Rocky Mountain woodlands from lodgepole groves to Engelmann spruces, plus meadowlands, lakes, and alpine terrain awaiting hikers who go farther.

Starting at 8,500 feet, the Wild Basin Trail is ideal for introductory hiking or backpacking in Colorado because it lacks the challenge of acclimatization to higher elevations. Busy as it is, this part of the park is less crowded than other trailheads that become mobbed; rangers close the entire park's gates on the busiest days. Go in late summer or early fall to miss the rush in this third-most-visited national park.

Start at the end of Wild Basin's gravel road and walk the trail west 1.5 miles. Go left at the first junction, right at the second to Ouzel Falls, and then 2.2 miles to Ouzel Lake or 3.4 miles to Bluebird Lake. Overnight permits are required; apply early.

From Estes Park, take Highway 7 south 13 miles, turn west on Wild Basin Road, and drive 2 miles on gravel to the Ouzel Lake Trailhead. In summer, the large lot fills by 8:00 a.m., requiring you to park along the dusty road.

Hundreds of hikes in national forests of Colorado and neighboring states take you to similar forests. Exceptionally large ponderosa pines, Douglas firs, and blue spruces are rare in the Rockies owing to frequent fire cycles, logging, and harsh conditions, but these three species grow to heights of 161, 160, and 181 feet respectively in remote off-trail locations of the Hermosa Creek drainage in southwest Colorado's San Juan Mountains. Massive cottonwoods are found along many riverfronts—some easily reached in frontcountry or urban edges, such as Boulder Creek through the city of Boulder.

Avalanche Creek Trail, White River National Forest

LOCATION
south of Carbondale

LENGTH
1 to 6 miles out and back or more

DIFFICULTY
moderate to strenuous, high elevation

TREE SPECIES
aspens, black cottonwoods, lodgepole pines, Engelmann spruces

HIGHLIGHTS
aspen groves, black cottonwood riparian forest

Aspen groves are a signature of sunny Rocky Mountain slopes from New Mexico to Canada, but especially in Colorado. Here, a grove of the clonal species fills a sunny pocket at the runout of an avalanche zone among Engelmann spruces, while a mountain alder greens the understory along Avalanche Creek Trail.

OPPOSITE: Along Avalanche Creek, black cottonwoods crown the floodplain forest of the Rockies. These and other cottonwood species are among the tallest and largest broadleaf trees on the continent.

Colorado is famous for aspens in pure stands of nearly white trunks filling the view, green leaves perpetually "quaking" in the slightest breeze and turning famously yellow and orange when autumn chills the slopes. This hike in White River National Forest features those trees well.

The trail ascends gradually, with water bubbling off flanks of Mount Sopris—a landmark to the north—and from eastward headwaters on Snowmass Mountain. Black cottonwoods with fat trunks highlight the first miles while aspens converge at avalanche chutes and meadows. Backpackers can continue to highcountry conifers and krummholz.

From I-70 at Glenwood Springs, drive Highway 82 south to Carbondale, then take Route 133 south 13 miles to an obscure left on 3D Road to Avalanche Creek Campground and the trailhead. On Route 133, Redstone is 5 miles too far.

Kamas Lake Trail, Uinta Mountains

UTAH

LOCATION
east of Salt Lake City

LENGTH
3 miles out and back

DIFFICULTY
easy, but high elevation

TREE SPECIES
lodgepole pines, Engelmann spruces, subalpine firs

HIGHLIGHTS
high Rocky Mountain forest and meadows

This high-elevation trail provides easy access at the interface of the Wasatch Range running north-south through Utah and the Uinta Mountains on their east-west axis between Salt Lake City and Colorado. Conifers with flowered meadows and breezy lakeshores combine for an artistic mix.

From Salt Lake City, take I-80 east to Silver Creek Junction and turn south on Highway 40. At Route 248, go east to Kamas and then onward on Route 150 (Mirror Lake Byway, closed in winter) arcing east and then north. Pass Mirror Lake, and in another mile park at Pass Lake Trailhead on the left. Hike north to Kamas Lake, with loop and longer possibilities. For more information, see the Uinta-Wasatch-Cache National Forest map.

The Rocky Mountains rise along the Kamas Lake Trail at the western limits of the Uinta Range with its domed and pointed summits. Lodgepole pines thrive in the foreground and subalpine firs, with obelisk tops, are shaped to shed snow at high elevations. Indian paintbrush and false hellebore texture the foreground.

Spring Mountains, Humboldt-Toiyabe National Forest

LOCATION
west of Las Vegas

LENGTH
1-mile loop

DIFFICULTY
easy, but high elevation

TREE SPECIES
bristlecone pines

HIGHLIGHTS
some of the world's oldest trees

Bristlecone groves are an arboreal highlight of the West, but they're found only in isolated remote sites at high elevations in dryland states: southeastern California, Nevada, southern Utah, and southwestern Colorado. One of the best and most accessible groves lies in Great Basin National Park, where the revered pines endure at the base of Wheeler Peak's soaring glacier-cleft rise.

OPPOSITE: The oldest trees in the world, bristlecone pines stand timelessly in the Spring Mountains. The Bristlecone Trail loops through this sublime grove where the trees we see today have withstood rigors of their high, severe sites for thousands of years.

This grove of ancient pines in Humboldt-Toiyabe National Forest thrives in the lofty Spring Mountains, which rake unexpected snowfall from storms over southern Nevada within sight of arid Las Vegas, whose neon grandiosity is miniaturized below. Via paved road, this is the easiest way to reach bristlecones—otherwise remote across their four-state region.

Bristlecones live longer than any other trees on earth, and that means any other *thing* on earth. Historically, some survived 5,000 years. Even after that, the trees' ecosystem role and beauty persist; trees have stood upright for 2,000 years *after dying*! These pines are found only on spare dry slopes and ridges of the Great Basin Province from the White Mountains of southeastern California to lonely ridges in Nevada, outposts in southern Utah, and southwestern Colorado.

The Spring Mountains grove is exceptional, with an interpretive trail at 8,470 feet looping through the elegantly austere forest. To avoid inflicting damage in this fragile setting, stay on the path.

From Las Vegas, drive Highway 95 north, continue past Route 157/Kyle Canyon Road, and go west on Route 156/Lee Canyon Road. Pass McWilliams and Dolomite Campgrounds, and park at Bristlecone Trailhead.

For another bristlecone trail near a paved road, visit Utah's Cedar Breaks National Monument. And if driving Highway 50 across Nevada, pause at Great Basin National Park near the Utah line for one of the best bristlecone trails at the base of Wheeler Peak.

Gila River, Gila National Forest

NEW MEXICO

LOCATION
north of Silver City

LENGTH
12-mile loop

DIFFICULTY
moderate to difficult because
of brush and fords

PRIMARY TREES
sycamores, Fremont
cottonwoods

HIGHLIGHTS
massive sycamores, wild
canyon river

The Gila River and its surrounding mountains constitute one of the largest and finest complexes of wildlands south of the Greater Yellowstone Ecosystem. The Middle Fork hike features Arizona sycamores with bleached white bark and sky-reaching limbs over floodplains.

This unusual hike ascends the Middle Fork Gila River and its wilderness in Gila National Forest, passing statuesque sycamores and cottonwoods shading the dryland's riparian community.

Sycamore bark mottles in camouflage-like blotches of tan, green, and brown, while younger branches bleach pure white and angular limbs reach skyward across a parched rocky landscape. These are Arizona sycamores, whose leaves—unlike California and eastern sycamores—are less toothed and the bark is noticeably whiter, as if selected for heat reflection. Fremont cottonwoods also rise high, casting appreciated shade.

With the Southwest's wildest river as a center-piece, Gila was the first wilderness administratively safeguarded by the Forest Service when the revered biologist Aldo Leopold worked here and championed protection in 1924. Several forks drain the Mogollon Mountains. These and four adjacent ranges consti-tute the largest block of mountain and forest terrain in New Mexico and a wildland core comparable in its own regional importance to the Greater Yellowstone Ecosystem of the middle Rockies. Issues of protec-tion have lingered since Leopold's day; irrigators proposed diversions from the river farther west in a plan that finally appears to be thwarted by the state's withdrawal of support in 2020. A protection cam-paign seeks to designate part of this stellar stream as a national wild and scenic river.

Drive to the Gila Cliff Dwellings Monument visitor center at the Middle Fork Gila River. The path winds 7 miles up to the Little Bear Canyon Trail junction and requires 32 fords (take walking sticks!) where the Middle Fork repeatedly encounters cliffs; wading is central to the experience here. To com-plete the loop, go south (left) at Little Bear Canyon

Trail, cross a low divide to the Gila's West Fork, turn left at the road, and walk 1 paved mile back to the visitor center.

Beware that floods wash out the Middle Fork path in places. The thigh-deep fords are easy at low-medium levels. To minimize stream damage, cross directly and avoid walking up and down the channel. Don't go when the river's up or rainstorms threaten—typically in the monsoon season of mid- to late summer—as hikers have been stranded. Avoid cold weather because you'll inevitably be wet. And, by the way, don't forget about rattle-snakes. Late spring is beautiful for hiking provided the stream is not high. Summer is hot, but monsoon rains may interfere.

From Silver City, take Highway 15 (West Fork Scenic Byway) north 43 miles to the visitor center.

Along the Gila River Trail in springtime, a Fremont cottonwood reaches boldly for the moisture-free sky.

Oak Creek Canyon

ARIZONA

LOCATION
north of Sedona

LENGTH
1 to 6 miles out and back

DIFFICULTY
easy to strenuous

TREE SPECIES
Arizona sycamores, Arizona
alders, ponderosa pines

HIGHLIGHTS
riparian forest, sycamores

Popular stream walks lie at the doorstep of the bustling resort town of Sedona and reveal a watery oasis in forested canyons dropping toward the Verde River and hot country below.

Hiking here features Arizona sycamores beautifully articulated against blue skies, plus alders and ponderosa pines backed by red-rock walls that veritably glow in canyon-filtered light. Access points occur along 12 miles of Highway 89A through the 1,000-foot-deep canyon.

For the popular and more challenging West Fork hike, take Highway 89A north 10 miles from Sedona. Between mileposts 385 and 384, turn west on a paved driveway to the trail—maintained for 3 miles but then less defined and requiring fords. Beware of high or rising water.

Except for wading, hiking is fine in winter and beautiful in spring and autumn. Summer is hot, but the water cools.

From Sedona, drive north on Highway 89A, park at creek-side pullouts, and explore paralleling paths. For the West Fork adventure, take a Coconino National Forest map.

Oak Creek Canyon is the second-most popular tourist draw in Arizona after the Grand Canyon, so visits here are best in off-hours and the shoulder seasons of early spring and late fall. Permian-aged red sandstone walls of the Schnebly Hill Formation are a backdrop for the green of Douglas firs in the canyon along Highway 89A.

Organ Pipe Cactus National Monument

ARIZONA

LOCATION
Mexican border south of Gila Bend

LENGTH
1 mile and more

DIFFICULTY
easy to strenuous

TREE SPECIES
organ pipe cacti, saguaro, paloverde

HIGHLIGHTS
Mojave Desert vegetation

Saguaro cacti thrive at Organ Pipe Cactus National Monument and other sites across the Sonoran Desert. Protected in relatively small preserves, the stately saguaros are threatened by suburban development and exotic grasses that have usurped native ground cover and burn readily beneath the saguaros, which evolutionarily saw few fires and are maladapted to them.

OPPOSITE: At Organ Pipe Cactus National Monument, xeric plants and harshly jagged peaks can be seen on the Desert View Trail. The endemic organ pipe cacti, shown here, are a highlight of this park and found nowhere else in the wild.

For the ultimate desert—and desert "forest"—Organ Pipe Cactus National Monument is the place. Strolls here take you to tall spires of saguaro cacti with their uplifted arms in classic Mojave mode. The park's namesake, organ pipe cactus, grows trunks similar to saguaro but shorter, with multiple stems vaguely resembling organ pipes. Beyond that noted endemic, the park—a UNESCO world heritage site—features a suite of prickly plant life not seen in other regions.

It may be a stretch to call the saguaro a "tree," as its trunks, leaves, vascular system, and appearance are distinctly different from any deciduous or coniferous species, yet these cacti are upright, tall,

and woody. Accordion-like "bark" swells with water absorbed during the infrequent rains, and the cacti's pleats expand with stored fluid to last through extended droughts when annual precipitation can total only a few inches, if that.

At the visitor center, grab a map and select your paths through the cacti forest. Try the mile-long Desert View and Arch Canyon Trails. Estes Canyon makes a 3-mile round trip. If you are fit and ready for heat, climb from Estes Canyon-Bull Pasture Trailhead to Ajo Peak, immediately east.

Here, and in all desert areas, avoid walking on the ubiquitous, blackened, upraised cryptogamic soil—not just dirt but a living crust of lichens and mixed biota essential to soil protection and the ecosystem. Stay on trails, walk in washes and on bedrock, or step stone to stone.

Issues of illegal crossing and safety at the Mexican border closed the monument in the 1990s, but with precautions in place the park reopened in 2014, and the Park Service considers hiking on park trails safe. Avoid unofficial paths. Embroiled in controversy, a Trump Administration border "wall" was under construction within the park in 2020, with wide swaths of cacti being leveled and with watershed and habitat disturbance.

This is a great place to go during the depths of winter on balmy days, or most anytime, October through March. Otherwise expect intense temperatures and beware of heatstroke.

From I-8 halfway between Tucson and California, take exit 116 at Gila Bend and drive south on Highway 85 to the monument's visitor center.

For other saguaro trails and winter delights, visit Saguaro National Park's two units east and west of Tucson.

CALIFORNIA

California has alpine forests, oaks in savannas at the bases of the Sierra Nevada and Coast Ranges, North Coast woodlands with more conifer species than any other place on the continent, and redwoods occupying a class by themselves. And that's just scratching the surface.

This variety reflects the state's transition zones: from one of the wettest places in America, near Oregon, to the driest, bordering Nevada, and from the highest point in 49 states—14,505-foot Mount Whitney—to the lowest, 282 feet below sea level in Death Valley. Trees respond to mandates of geography, giving us forests as remarkable as the landforms beneath them—wetlands to volcanoes. One could take an arboreal vacation here by touring a different ecosystem every day for a week or two.

Where other regions no doubt have special intricacies of life, their forests might seem similar for hundreds of miles. Here at the West Coast, distinct forests often arise within short jaunts to the next mountain or valley. Scenes quickly transform: seacoast to savanna, foothill to high-country, desert in fragrant bloom to ridgeline buried under snow.

A list of forest destinations might begin with the state's superlatives. Bristlecone pines in the White Mountains are the oldest trees worldwide. Giant sequoias in the Sierra Nevada are the largest. Coast redwoods in summer fog are the tallest. Valley oaks, with their girth, muscular limbs, and cathedral-like domes of foliage overhead, are the most iconic trees in Californian culture, from John Steinbeck novels onward. Joshua trees are brazenly bizarre, with prickly arms twisting toward arid indigo skies. Fabulous sycamores, madrones, firs, pines, and palms all await.

Consider the Sierra Nevada alone: the western foothills of these mountains begin in grasslands cut by rivers lined with cottonwoods and buckeyes, roll upward into an oak savanna on hills emerald in spring but golden brown the rest of the year, go onward to columnar ponderosa pines, and further into uplands with groves of resinous-scented conifers more picturesque than any others on earth. Trunks of stout junipers sometimes seem as wide as their height. Cones of sugar pines reach 20 inches in length. And speaking of cones, Coulter pines in California's coastal mountains produce intimidatingly spiked cones that outweigh a pineapple at 8 pounds.

California is trail-rich, with thousands of miles of pathways fingering through the mountain ranges and with a system of national parks, national forests, and state parks that totals 52 percent of the West's largest state. It is unmatched for accessibility to hikers. Protecting at least half the landscape is what conservation biologists recommend for ecosystem functions and survival of native species everywhere. Public-land status here might well be considered a model for other states, though much remains to be done to truly protect what is public and to add critical missing elements to the safeguarded ecosystem inventory.

California's forests are also at the painful edge of unfolding tragedies. Urbanization remains intense in this most-populated state. Logging pressures have been extreme since the gold rush. A disease called sudden oak death plagues forests in the north, while ozone cripples trees windward from southern freeways and Central Valley cities. Fires rage across landscapes desiccated by global warming, occurring with annual regularity in ways never before seen. Fortunately, California also has the most vigorous environmental movement in America, with organizations like Save the Redwoods League and the California Wilderness Coalition striving to save the best that's left and nurture an economy based on intrinsic wealth instead of commodification and endless growth.

No surprise in this state known for sunshine, the season for exploring lasts all year, but that depends on where you go. See desert regions in late winter before temperatures top triple digits. Coastal areas remain vernal-like across the calendar, but April is spectacular when a burst of green and riot of wildflowers make for days of heaven. Summer is delightful in the highcountry of the Sierra, though the smoke of climate-crisis fires increasingly interferes with walks in the woods. Autumn is delectable in those mountains and in northern ranges, with nighttime chills relieving summer's heat.

Forest hikes are covered here first with the White Mountains to the southeast. Then we'll jump to the dominant mountain range, the Sierra Nevada, running 400 miles south to north. Next, we'll go to the coastal mountains in the southern part of the state, migrate to the Central Coast, and then move onward to Northern California forests blending inland.

Schulman Grove, Inyo National Forest

LOCATION
east of Bishop

LENGTH
5-mile loop, with shorter or longer hikes

DIFFICULTY
moderate to strenuous, very high elevation

TREE SPECIES
bristlecone pines, limber pines, single-leaf pinyons

HIGHLIGHTS
oldest trees anywhere

Some forest aficionados put the pilgrimage to this remote grove at the top of their list, as these are the oldest trees on earth. And they look it. Contorted, microscopically grained, and still-living bristlecones date back 4,000 years and more. Spare conditions high in the White Mountains along the Nevada border protect these hardy trees from fires, browsers, insects, and wet-weather rot. Trees that we can walk to and see have been growing since the Stone Age—they are living relics of the prehistoric past, like meeting a mastodon, saber-toothed tiger, or caveman on the trail.

Bristlecones thrive on dolomite—calcareous alkaline rock found on scattered ridges at lofty elevations here and at similar heights scattered eastward to Colorado. Many of the bristlecones retain only a limb or two of living tissue, otherwise bleached and weathered by the elements. The location of the Methuselah Tree—estimated at 4,852 years old in 2020—is undisclosed to avoid vandalism. But many ancient bristlecones stand in quite well, worthy of deepest reverence for the oldest of life.

Limber pines, hardly less charismatic in their ancient growth, accompany the bristlecones. The paved-road approach to the Schulman Grove also passes through pure stands of single-leaf pinyon

and Utah juniper—common small trees throughout upper elevations of the Great Basin, which extends from here eastward and into the Rocky Mountain foothills.

Near the visitor center, stroll the Methuselah Grove Trail, looping through highcountry with rarefied air. Here, at an elevation of 9,800 feet, some people may have trouble; return to lower ground if you have an extreme headache or other signs of altitude sickness.

For more bristlecones, drive another 12 miles on a rough dirt road to the Patriarch Grove—even higher at 11,300 feet—with its mile-long trail.

The Schulman road doesn't open until mid-May or so, and closes before December. Fall is glorious but sharply cold when not in sunshine; I've been surprised with temperatures of 10 degrees at daybreak just down the road from the grove. Winter is severe and the road unplowed, but the bristlecones can tempt capable backcountry skiers in springtime when the days warm but consolidated wind-packed snow persists.

From Bishop, drive south on Highway 395 for 15 miles to Big Pine. Turn east on Route 168, go 12 miles, turn left on White Mountain Road, and drive 10 miles to the visitor center.

PREVIOUS SPREAD: In the redwoods of Northern California, the Stout Memorial Grove Trail in Jedediah Smith Redwoods State Park offers an easy half-mile stroll, reached in summer and fall via a footbridge over the Smith River.

The bristlecone pines of the Schulman Grove in Inyo National Forest are the oldest trees on earth.

Kearsarge Pass, Inyo National Forest

CALIFORNIA

LOCATION
south of Bishop

LENGTH
8 miles out and back

DIFFICULTY
strenuous, high elevation

TREE SPECIES
foxtail pines, willows

HIGHLIGHTS
foxtail pines and other high Sierra conifers

For some conifer aficionados, a hike to foxtail pines is a must. These lesser-known but captivating evergreens can live 700 to 2,000 years in their lean environs near timberline in the Sierra Nevada, and seeing them takes some effort. One route to their lofty stronghold is Kearsarge Pass Trail.

Foxtails allure here with their seniority, golden bark, hefty diameters to six feet, and austere settings. With bottlebrush needle clusters, they appear to be first cousins of bristlecone pines, and are; some botanists theorize that pollen has blown 20 miles between the two species and hybridized, according to John D. Stuart and John O. Sawyer's *Trees and Shrubs of California*.

The trail ascends 4 miles to the Sierra Crest. Be ready for the rocky tread and thin air if you go to the pass, with its breathtaking view west to Kings River headwaters. Though 11,700 feet high and no pushover, Kearsarge is one of the easiest and shortest ways to access the highcountry of the southeastern Sierra—a good bang for the buck in reaching upper-level conifers. So expect other hikers.

Snow lingers until July, and summer is hot. Autumn is total enchantment here and elsewhere on the east side of the Sierra.

From Highway 395 at Bishop, drive south to Independence. Turn west in the middle of town, ascend Onion Valley Road, stay right, and switchback to the end.

Other trails climb to starkly beautiful conifer forests from multiple trailheads on the east side of the Sierra—between Cottonwood Lakes Trailhead near Lone Pine in the south and aspen-brightened Lundy Canyon near Mono Lake in the north.

Surviving the ages in spare terrain, foxtail pines boldly border the Kearsarge Pass Trail with University Peak filling the background.

OPPOSITE: Charismatic foxtail pines hide at high elevations in the southeastern Sierra Nevada, typically remote from trailheads. This grove is reached via the Kearsarge Pass Trail with an uphill climb of 2 miles.

Eastman Lake Oaks

CALIFORNIA

LOCATION
north of Fresno and Madera

LENGTH
1 to 3 miles

DIFFICULTY
easy

TREE SPECIES
California live oaks, blue oaks

HIGHLIGHTS
large oak trees, oak savanna at Sierra Nevada foothills

Valley and blue oaks at Eastman Lake rise from the grassland savanna that greens up vividly in springtime. Trails, volunteer footpaths, and free-form wanderings lead to these capable hardwoods among volcanic rock outcrops of the Sierra Nevada foothills.

Upslope from an Army Corps of Engineers reservoir that no doubt flooded a lot of remarkable trees, this low-key recreation area includes a rolling expanse of elegant oak savanna, much the way hundreds of miles once existed through Sierra Nevada foothills above the flats of California's Central Valley but below the chaparral and pine-dotted rise of big mountains eastward.

Valley oaks reach diameters of three feet and more with round-toothed leaves like miniature foliage of white oaks, while blue oaks are smaller in stature with wavy-leaf edges. Both spread their umbrella crowns across a sea of grass and wildflowers. In April and May, shrubby lupines complement the green with blue flowers. Paths and free-form wandering lead to elegant clusters of oaks and toothy outcrops of underlying limestone. I've found the most beautiful trees north from the reservoir.

Early springtime is best, when grass greens up brilliantly and medleys of flowers burst into bloom. Unfortunately, the shallow-rooted, exotic annual grasses that long ago invaded with cattle have replaced the deep-rooted bunchgrasses and now dominate—morphing into a prickly brown fire hazard after April's vernal moisture dries and making walking less pleasant by June, let alone transforming an entire ecosystem to one of less abundance. Don't obsess, but beware of ticks in spring by checking yourself after walking, and of mice-eating rattlesnakes if you roam off-trail in summer, which is intensely hot.

From Highway 99 north of Fresno and Madera, take exit 170/Chowchilla, go east on Avenue 26 to the T, and then turn left on Route 29 to Eastman.

Giant Forest, Sequoia National Park

CALIFORNIA

LOCATION
east of Visalia

LENGTH
1-mile out and back,
and longer

DIFFICULTY
easy

TREE SPECIES
sequoias, sugar pines,
ponderosa pines, red firs

HIGHLIGHTS
largest trees on earth

The Giant Forest of Sequoia National Park is the premier grove for seeing the largest trees—and largest living organisms—on earth. Five of the 10 most massive sequoias live here, like this one, whose top disappears into the Sierra Nevada sky.

A visit to the sequoias ranks as one of the greatest forest pilgrimages one might take. This grove is eminently accessible from paved roads, but—beware—everyone wants to go there.

Though not the tallest or fattest sequoia, General Sherman here is the world's largest tree and largest living organism in total volume—27 feet in diameter, 274 feet tall, and at last count about 2,200 years old. As the runner-up, a tree known as Washington stands along a spur trail drawing comparatively few admirers. The Giant Forest has 8,000 sequoias, including five of the 10 largest.

Dwarfed in scale, but giants in their own right, sugar pines, ponderosa pines, Jeffrey pines, white firs, and red firs also impress anyone open to them.

Sequoias can live 3,000 years or longer, and like most trees, they continue to grow all their lives. And get this: because of their astounding girth, and the fact that the volume of a cylinder (tree trunk) increases not with its linear radius but with the *square* of its radius, a mature giant annually puts on the equivalent volume of a full tree 60 feet tall and one foot in diameter. Each year! (Remember? Volume equals pi times the radius squared times height.) In other words, even thin annual growth rings on a large tree can mean more volume of wood that's added each year than the amount occurring with larger-spaced rings on a small tree. The take-home message is this: in the age of global warming caused by atmospheric buildup of carbon dioxide, old-growth trees are veritable carbon-sequestering machines—as long as they're allowed to stand.

The trees and their native forest are fire adapted and fire dependent. Under natural conditions, flames walked through every five to 35 years,

burning fallen limbs and pruning invasive young trees but sparing the big ones with their golden brown, vertically fluted bark that thickens to 24 inches as a firewall guarding the living tissue beneath. The big trees' long boles—limb-free for 100 feet or more above ground—offer no intermediate fuel as "fire ladders," whereby flames can climb to the otherwise vulnerable crowns. Thus, the big trees have for ages been virtually fireproof.

But now climate change poses ominous threats. With the frost line retreating higher up the mountains, the sequoia zone still receives rain, but far less snow, and that reduces the runoff season and yields less water storage lingering in the soil. Hotter temperatures lead to reproductive dysfunction and troublesome ecological changes. Even worse, the intensity of recent fires—driven by high winds in scorching summers of the global-warming era—have damaged large sequoias historically not fazed by lower-intensity flames. Worse yet, according to Park Service reports in 2020, the hotter climate has allowed bark beetles to thrive and kill sequoias previously protected by the tree's sap-exuding defenses, which are now curtailed by more heat and less water.

Even with California's per capita air-pollution improvements spanning decades, the population growth and resulting pollution from traffic upwind has undermined those gains; the air is still rated "unhealthy" for park visitors two months each year, and it affects young sequoias as well.

Further reduction of pollution will help sustain these forests, yet conditions are poised to get worse. Oil- and gas-drilling fields to the west are part of the pollution problem, and plans in 2020 called for expansion of drilling on 1.2 million acres, including land near the park's western border. So see these trees while you can, and support broad-based ecological protection of their habitat and air supply.

The Giant Forest area has 40 miles of trails—many 1 to 5 miles long. The famous General Sherman Tree is reached by a 1-mile round trip from the parking lot—which was tastefully relocated from the previous site unnecessarily close to the great tree. The 2-mile paved Congress Trail passes many of the largest sequoias, including the clustered Senate Group of six. Get a map at the visitor center.

Beware, Giant Forest is a bustling tourist hub. Aim for shoulder seasons, early and late in the day, and even winter. The Park Service plows the road, and the sequoias' golden-barked, green-needled, two-toned beauty is wildly enhanced by the white outlines of snow. Conditions then may require chains; always carry them when approaching the Sierra in winter. Summer is hot but pleasant at this elevation; spring and fall are simply extraordinary.

Approaching from the south, take Route 99 to Visalia. Exit on Route 198 east, go right at Wolverton, and turn right into the General Sherman parking lot. From Fresno, take Highway 180 east into Kings Canyon National Park. At Grant Grove Village, turn right on the Generals Highway heading south into Sequoia Park, then left at Wolverton, and then right into the lot.

On the west slope of the Sierra between elevations of 5,000 and 7,000 feet, and from Sequoia National Forest in the south to Eldorado National Forest in the north, 75 native sequoia groves survive, mostly small, many remote. Sequoia and Kings Canyon National Parks form the heart of this big-tree zone.

Grant Grove, Kings Canyon National Park

CALIFORNIA

LOCATION
east of Fresno

LENGTH
0.5 miles or more

DIFFICULTY
easy

TREE SPECIES
sequoias, sugar pines, red firs

HIGHLIGHTS
some of the largest trees on earth

Twin to the Giant Forest grove that rises in the seamlessly adjoining Sequoia National Park, this grove of thousands of sequoias in Kings Canyon National Park includes the 3,000-year-old General Grant Tree. At 29 feet in diameter and 267 feet tall, it is the second-largest tree on earth.

A half-mile trail from the Grant Grove parking lot leads to the big tree and others. The North Grove Loop is 1.5 miles. The Redwood Canyon Trail is reached by driving 6 miles south and then turning right on a dirt road running 2 miles to the trailhead. Take off for the walk of your choice among 16 miles of paths.

From Fresno, drive east on Highway 180 to Kings Canyon National Park and the intersection of Highway 198 and Generals Highway. Turn right into the Grant Grove visitor center, or go directly to the Grant Tree parking lot 1 mile farther northwest.

At the Grant Grove, these four sequoias fill the space ahead like a solid wall of cellulose.

OPPOSITE: The Grant Grove of monumental trees rises in Kings Canyon National Park—just north from the Giant Forest of Sequoia National Park.

Yosemite Valley, Yosemite National Park

LOCATION
east of Modesto

LENGTH
0.5 miles or more

DIFFICULTY
easy

TREE SPECIES
ponderosa pines, lodgepole pines, California black oaks

HIGHLIGHTS
oaks and pines framing scenic views

Yosemite Valley can hardly be omitted from any accounting of nature in America, and its forests make it an American phenomenon of scenery almost as much as its famed waterfalls.

Part of the valley's charm is its elegant mingling of trees and meadows where shaded refuge is paired with expansive views—a sweet combination that geographer Jay Appleton called "prospect and refuge" serving humankind in evolutionarily important ways: we've benefited from places that offered both prospects, so we can see what might be threatening on the horizon, and also refuge for safety. Such practical advantages to survival instilled aesthetic preferences that we still feel today. Touching these concepts, perimeter paths around Yosemite's open spaces make for dreamy arboreal strolls unlike any others, where one can feel the shelter of the forest but still see the spectacular view beyond.

Walk the meadow paths at the base of El Capitan's cliff face at the west end of the valley, and, my favorite, the perimeter trail around Leidig Meadow in the center of the valley west of Yosemite Valley Lodge. California black oaks and ponderosa pines are captivating there and elsewhere. Most Yosemite trails also have memorable incense cedars.

Yosemite Valley is seductive, but hot in summer and the crowds are intense—4.6 million people visited in 2019. But early morning and evening walks can enchant even on mobbed days. Try for spring and fall; there is good weather in May, September, and October. Even those months are busy, making risky if not foul weather in March and November tempting.

Also in Yosemite, the Mariposa Grove of sequoias—home of the Grizzly Giant, 28 feet thick—lies at the park's southern end; take Wawona Road/Route 41 south from Yosemite Valley past the Wawona Hotel and turn left. Meanwhile, the Tuolumne Grove of sequoias and sugar pines lies northwest of the valley; take Big Oak Flat Road west to Crane Flat, turn right on Tioga Road/Route 120, and continue to the left-side turnoff.

To round out Yosemite's forest attractions, visit Tuolumne Meadows in the park's northern reaches, wander alpine meadows, and hike into the Grand Canyon of the Tuolumne, with its lodgepole pines, red firs, and incense cedars.

From California's Central Valley, drive Route 120 to the park from the north or Route 140 from the south.

A stroll through Yosemite Valley visits ponderosa pines and California black oaks that ring the meadows and frame the national park's famous views. Acorns from these and other oak species were primary foods for local Native Americans and remain so for deer, small mammals, and acorn woodpeckers, who store the nutty seeds in storage holes they cleverly drill in tree trunks nearby.

Calaveras Big Trees State Park

LOCATION
east of Angels Camp

LENGTH
0.5 to 5 miles

DIFFICULTY
easy to moderate

TREE SPECIES
sequoias, sugar pines, ponderosa pines, Pacific dogwoods

HIGHLIGHTS
sequoia grove, mixed conifers

While the legendary sequoia groves in the national parks southward get top billing, sequoias, companion sugar pines, and other conifers join to create a state park of impressive stature here. Trails tour two sequoia groves, and the park includes the conifer-lined shores of the North Fork Stanislaus River and its foaming whitewater. Closest to the entrance, a 1.5-mile nature trail loops through the North Grove. Then, drive 5 miles to the 5-mile South Grove Trail, which reaches the park's two largest trees.

Summer is hot but pleasant. Fall is glorious with Pacific dogwoods in scarlet and orange, while in spring the dogwoods burst in white blooms. The entrance is open in winter, with the opportunity to see the golden-barked sequoias decked out in crystals after low-elevation snowstorms, which are increasingly rare but special if you're prepared and catch one.

From California's Central Valley at Stockton, take Route 4 to Angels Camp and continue 23 miles.

A Pacific dogwood lightens the scene at Calaveras Big Trees State Park beneath a trio of giant sequoias.

OPPOSITE: The Calaveras sequoia groves lie north of the famous big trees of Yosemite, Kings Canyon, and Sequoia National Parks, but they are scarcely less awesome in their size and setting among forest wonders. Fresh snow fell here at the North Grove and not even a single footprint tracked the path ahead. As impressive in its own way, a sugar pine—largest of the pine family—rises on the right.

Sonora and Ebbetts Passes

These two Sierra Nevada passes are superb places to step out of the car and tour the mix of high-elevation forest typically reached only with long hikes. Each pass offers a splendid gallery of climate-shaped, wind-sculpted trees enduring the ages at elevations beyond usual threats of fire, insects, and logging.

The more southern Sonora Pass has clusters of whitebark pines producing crops of pine nuts essential to jay-like Clark's nutcrackers and to bears that ferret out some of the birds' nut caches during autumn's feeding frenzy preceding hibernation. Dense groves of ancient bleached white snags of whitebarks are seen with a rigorous climb south of the pass to ridgelines beyond Leavitt Peak. Other striking scenes come with lodgepole pines in starkly weathered forms and, alternatively, in robust groves at the edge of snowbanks persisting in early summer. On the western approach to the pass, the largest known Jeffrey pine—the Eureka Giant—stands near the Columns of the Giants lava formation in Stanislaus National Forest.

Ebbetts Pass is the next highway crossing northward. It hosts a suite of highcountry conifers, but specializes in western junipers with stout iterations locally known as Sierra junipers, prominent along the Pacific Crest Trail north of the pass. The junipers live thousands of years and their rigid bulwarks of gnarly limbs enliven spare rocky slopes.

Near both passes and at slightly lower elevations, elegant western white pines grow to immense boles, Jeffrey pines wear golden bark fractured like pieces of a jigsaw puzzle, and red firs in corrugated maroon-brown bark monopolize steep mountainsides.

The Pacific Crest Trail tracks through both passes on its 2,650-mile route from Mexico to

LOCATION
east of Sonora and Angels Camp

LENGTH
short or long

DIFFICULTY
easy to strenuous, high elevation

TREE SPECIES
Sierra (western) junipers, whitebark pines, red firs, lodgepole pines, Jeffrey pines, red firs

HIGHLIGHTS
highcountry conifers

With winter's snow still deep in the backcountry of Ebbetts Pass, lodgepole pines have twisted through the ages in upward spirals and await the next Sierra Nevada storm that brews with promise on the horizon. The Sierra lodgepoles grow to three-foot diameters and 100-foot heights as outsized subspecies of the lodgepoles that form thickets of smaller, arrow-straight trees in the Rocky Mountains.

At Sonora Pass, the moon rises over a grove of lodgepole pines whose trunks catch the last warmth of sunset.

OPPOSITE: Living up to 3,000 years, Sierra junipers appear at high elevations where they often cling to cliffs with roots deeply embedded in cracks. This one endures at Carson Pass—the next highway crossing north of Ebbetts Pass.

Canada, and it makes an arterial path for both day hikes and epic outings by walking either north or south from each pass.

This is California, so crowds are an issue anywhere there is easy access. Consider visiting in autumn when the air is crisp, or in early June, as soon as the passes open, when the wonders of winter combine with the comforts of spring, all revealed by backcountry skiing, snowshoeing, or simply hiking on top of the snow, which by then is mostly consolidated enough for walking on top with nominal breakthrough.

From California's Central Valley at Manteca, take Route 108 east through Sonora and on to Sonora Pass; park at the top or pullouts along the way. For Ebbetts Pass, take Route 4 from Stockton east through Angels Camp to the pass. Both passes, and Tioga Pass to the south, are closed from November to May and sometimes later.

Similar highcountry forests can be found in all Sierra Nevada passes crossed by the state highway system. Carson Pass lies north of Ebbetts Pass, drivable year-round on Route 88, with excellent hiking, especially to the south. Rewards are even better via remote passes and peaks reached only by trail.

For skiers or snowshoers, roadside parking lots throughout the Sierra Nevada require Sno-Park stickers from November to April; they are for sale in outdoor shops and local stores. This is how the state pays to plow the parking lots.

Joshua Tree National Park

LOCATION
east of San Bernardino

LENGTH
1 mile or more

DIFFICULTY
easy to moderate

TREE SPECIES
Joshua trees, California fan palms

HIGHLIGHTS
Mojave Desert, palm oasis

In Southern California, just east of the Peninsular and Coast Ranges that rake moisture from Pacific storms, Joshua Tree National Park is home to the largest members of the yucca family. Twilights of red sky are common here as the sun drops west of the Los Angeles air basin. Botanists tragically project that most Joshua trees in this finest of all groves will fail to endure the warming climate and increased fires it brings.

While saguaro cacti typify the Sonoran Desert to the east, Southern California's Mojave Desert is emblematized by Joshua trees. Their contorted trunks, twisted arms, and sword-bristling foliage whimsically arise from severe landscapes, and the flowers and treelike structure provide food and shelter in harsh terrain. Joshua trees are a keystone species on which many others depend for blossoms, roots, seed husks, and habitat.

See these beautifully bizarre iterations of trees while they're here; the warming climate is expected to eliminate nearly all Joshua trees in the park by the end of this century. Virtually none are reproducing. Even the best-case scenario shows an 80 percent loss. Biologists reporting in *Ecosphere* in June 2019 found that the trees will succumb to heat and wildfires, which are intensifying with the invasion of exotic grasses that thrive in the polluted, nitrogen-rich air of Southern California. Wetter winters don't always help, as they spur more growth of encroaching flammable grasses that fuel even hotter wildfires when the inevitable dry months arrive. With cooler microclimates, lesser groves of a separate Joshua tree species survive, for now, to the east at higher elevations in Nevada and Arizona—hardly a substitute for the magnificent Joshuas currently in California.

Stop at the visitor center and select a trail, say, Jumbo Rocks. Though lacking picturesque Joshua trees, a longer route climbs to Lost Palms Oasis— a true desert oasis with springflows nourishing California fan palms and birds in foliage overhead.

From Los Angeles, take I-10 east past San Bernardino. At Highway 62, turn north to Yucca Valley and then south at the park entrance.

While in the neighborhood, due south of Palm Springs is an intriguing riparian forest of California

fan palms that shades Indian Canyons of the Agua Caliente Indian Reservation. From Palm Springs, take South Palm Canyon Drive south, enter the reservation ($9 in 2020), and turn right to Andreas Canyon and its 1-mile loop trail along the palm-crowded stream. October through April is best here and at Joshua Tree.

OPPOSITE: Not far from Joshua Tree National Park, another striking forest of the California desert rises with fan palms in the streamside oasis of Palm Canyon, which is on the Agua Caliente Indian Reservation south of Palm Springs.

This bizarre assemblage of Joshua trees near Quail Springs in Joshua Tree National Park makes for one of the most unusual American forests. Rock climbers flock to the bulbous granite outcrops, especially in winter, when other climbing areas are iced over.

Point Mugu State Park

CALIFORNIA

LOCATION
northwest of Los Angeles,
southeast of Oxnard

LENGTH
2 miles out and back or more

DIFFICULTY
easy

TREE SPECIES
California sycamores, coast
live oaks

HIGHLIGHTS
sculptural sycamores

Principally a land of chaparral, the coast of Southern California is not often invoked for its great forests, but the trees of Sycamore Canyon at the western end of the Santa Monica Mountains are exceptional.

At Point Mugu State Park's Sycamore Canyon Campground, admire the intriguing artistry of these trees and see their organic architecture curving skyward. From Highway 1, enter the park and turn directly into the campground or go a bit farther to the trailhead.

Walk up the wide canyon bottom with gentle gradient along the intermittent stream, wet in winter. A 1-mile stroll to the Serrano Trail turnoff makes a fine tour, or continue up the canyon another 6 miles one way to its headwall at the park's Satwiwa Native American Culture Center. The trail there connects to a maze of others leading to the rugged Backbone Trail and southward to the Santa Monica Mountains' highest summit, 3,111-foot Sandstone Peak, which offers fabulous views across a sea of chaparral scribed with thin riparian tree corridors out to the ocean.

Closer to Los Angeles in the Santa Monica Mountains, equally large sycamores grace the streambanks of Malibu Creek State Park off Malibu Canyon Road.

California sycamores populate the canyon floor at Point Mugu State Park, where the western end of the Santa Monica Mountains ramps down to the sea and then disappears under water until reemerging offshore as the northern Channel Islands. The regular patterns of holes in the aged tree here are excavated by yellow-bellied sapsuckers.

Plaskett Creek and McWay Canyon

CALIFORNIA

LOCATION
south of Carmel

LENGTH
1 to 8 miles

DIFFICULTY
strenuous

PRIMARY TREES
coast live oaks, California
sycamores

HIGHLIGHTS
great trees on grassy slopes
overlooking the ocean,
redwoods

One among several climaxes of California coastal scenery occurs along Big Sur—an 80-mile shoreline where the Santa Lucia Mountains plunge from skyward heights into the sea between San Simeon in the south and Carmel in the north. Forest trails intrigue with the mystique of this revered coastline where tumultuous forces of nature are everywhere evident and always playing out.

Here, in America's most classic mountains-meet-sea landscape, winter storms drench the peaks in rain, and cool ocean winds deliver fog that dampens seaward slopes and canyons. Needing that fog in summer, the southernmost redwoods rise at Redwood Creek, pungent bay trees cast deep shade, coast live oaks grow burly, and sycamores arc over streamfronts and rock outcrops that concentrate and funnel runoff into root zones.

Enjoy a climb? Drive Highway 1 for 35 miles north from San Simeon to the heart of Big Sur at the Plaskett ranger station and walk the ridgeline trail north of the creek. This ascent tours a mix of grassland, forest groves, and majestic coast live oaks. An ambitious route continues around Plaskett Creek's canyon rim and loops back to the ranger station, but I've always been stonewalled by poison oak that thickens with grabby branches as the route bends south. In brushy areas, the viney, itchy "oak" is epidemic here, so stay on well-trod trails, but even there you have to watch for toxic branches fingering into your path. I also enjoy free-form walking on exhilarating grassy balds that veer up toward ridgelines and also plummet to the sea.

Spring is sensational with vivid green and wildflowers, but nothing is quite free; beware of ticks then.

For another Big Sur forest hike, see the southernmost large redwoods. From Carmel, drive 37 miles

Coast live oaks reach immense girth while living for centuries in the pruning winds and nourishing rainstorms of the Pacific coast. Acorns here are important to dozens of bird and mammal species. This oak cluster grips the ridgeline north of Plaskett Creek.

south to Julia Pfeiffer Burns State Park (*not* Pfeiffer Big Sur State Park, but 12 miles south of it). Park at the McWay Cove lot and walk the lesser-trod Ewoldsen Trail east and up, immediately entering redwoods, which increase in stature to crowns of 300 feet farther along the path. The loop clocks 4.6 miles round trip with a strenuous 1,600-foot climb if you go the distance. Cap the day off with a stroll to the McWay Falls overlook perched at the ocean's edge, where sunsets are outrageous.

OPPOSITE: Best known as the tallest trees in America, coast redwoods are found in ravines and canyons of the Big Sur coast, where fog coalesces against the foliage high above and then drips to the ground to nourish the trees' roots. The southernmost large redwood grove stands here in McWay Canyon of Julia Pfeiffer Burns State Park. Fog is especially important in summer because the shallow roots of the redwoods demand a yearlong water supply, yet the fog is diminishing with global and ocean warming.

California sycamores spread their limbs over the steep grassy slopes of the Big Sur coast near Plaskett Creek. Unlike most trees whose bark cracks and roughens, allowing the cambium within to grow, sycamores flake and shed patchy sections of bark, exposing younger layers emerging from within.

Milpitas Oaks

LOCATION
east of Big Sur, southwest of King City

LENGTH
1 mile or more

DIFFICULTY
easy, but harder to mountaintops

TREE SPECIES
valley oaks, sugar pines on Junipero Serra Peak

HIGHLIGHTS
savanna of statuesque oaks

One of the finest groves of giant valley oaks grow along Milpitas Road of the Fort Hunter Liggett Army Base, just inland from the Big Sur coast. Here, autumn's grass has long since browned with summer's drought, and November's low-angled afternoon sun warms the scene.

FOLLOWING SPREAD: In springtime, the Milpitas oak savanna greens with the juicy growth of grass and wildflowers thriving on winter rains that soak the ground from December to March of a wet year. Trails connect to Santa Lucia Range heights like the mountain seen in the background.

The lower and temperate elevations of California are a paradise of oaks in groves and savannas spanning from Mexico to Oregon and undulating inland to midelevation slopes of the Sierra Nevada. To me, this grove is the ultimate. Here, California's largest oak species shades and profiles a broad interior valley of the Santa Lucia Range, at once remote and accessible.

Oak woodlands might be considered the home habitat of Californians. Most places that people have settled are—or once were—sheltered by these trees. More than redwoods, more than mountains, even more than the signature Pacific shoreline, oak woodlands are California's native landscape where people live. And it's not just about us. Oak groves house more species of wildlife than any other vegetation type in the Golden State. Valley oaks grow 150 feet tall—even larger than the storied Virginia oaks of Deep South plantations. They hybridize with somewhat smaller blue oaks, which share a similar but more limited range across California's interior lowlands.

The beauty and presence of oaks in the Milpitas savanna belie the threats and plights that the seemingly indomitable trees face. Because of agriculture, firewood cutting, and development, valley oaks now occupy only 1.5 percent of their native range. More troubling, and owing to fundamental ecological transformations, relatively few of this species are germinating or surviving from their youth to reach a hearty and durable stature as a new generation. Culprits in the unfortunate chain of events are cattle, which were introduced en masse by early Spanish ranchers. Cows trample grasslands and compact the soil, they eat acorns and oak seedlings, and they brought with them

exotic annual grasses that displaced the deep-rooted native grasses that had been fundamental to ecosystem health. The exotics produce a surplus of seeds that feed gopher populations, which in turn consume more oak seedlings and acorns. In our never-ending talent for making matters worse, the near-religious elimination of rodent predators such as wolves and coyotes freed the troublesome rodents to boom in countless numbers. Meanwhile, fire suppression in an ecosystem that once burned frequently with low-level flames now encourages other plants that displace the oaks.

As if that weren't enough, a fungus-like pathogen, *Phytophthora ramorum*, has hitchhiked in with exotic nursery stock from Asia. It causes sudden oak death, which eliminates many trees in its wake. It targets coast live oaks and tanoaks, but also others, extending into southern Oregon. Meanwhile, a hotter climate makes regermination and survival difficult with intensified fire hazards rather than the lower-level flames of the past.

Fortunately, valley oaks and some related species can live 300 years, so survivors will hopefully not succumb to their multiple detractors soon. But a regenerative crop of trees has largely failed for the past century, according to botanists and the California Oak Foundation, and efforts to restore oaks at a landscape scale have been thwarted at every turn. Reestablishing ecological conditions more amenable to the trees' health and growth may be essential, such as eliminating cattle from critical areas, reintroducing top predators, managing low-level fires, and reinstating floods on floodplains where the valley oaks once excelled with the rivers' periodic overflow. Impediments to doing any of that are enormous. So see these great trees while you can. The protection of remaining oak groves through open-space acquisition is important and urgent for all who value these special woodlands.

At Milpitas, a few double-track lanes wind about, but the finest tour is done simply by strolling among the woody giants along volunteer footpaths.

Unusual for a natural area of this caliber, Milpitas is not a state or national park, but rather part of the Fort Hunter Liggett Army Base, and troops conduct exercises here. So restrictions of a temporary but mandatory nature may apply. However, I've always found the core road—Milpitas—to be open from the main access in the east and northward to Los Padres National Forest, where terrain steepens westward toward Cone Peak and northward toward Junipero Serra Peak. Both offer fine extended hikes.

Cone Peak rises to 5,155 feet within 3.4 miles of the sea—the highest summit so close to the Pacific Ocean south of Canada. Hiding farther inland, Junipero Serra Peak tops 5,856 feet—the highest in the Santa Lucia Range, and one of few places in California where I've seen a mountain lion. Trails climb each. Cone Peak has Coulter pines, with sharply spiked, weighty cones perched in the canopy like bombs. Fires have crisped the slopes in recent years, but the Coulters are serotinous, meaning fire dependent, and will regerminate. Junipero Serra's summit gleans snowfall in winter, which waters conifers like those found in the Sierra Nevada, including uplifted limbs of sugar pines, with their amazing foot-long cones that can stretch even larger.

Though inviting all year, spring is gorgeous here, when green grass dazzles and it's not too hot. But definitely check yourself for ticks at the end of the day.

From interior California, take Highway 101 to King City exit 282B. Turn west on Jolon Road, drive south 6 miles to Milpitas Road, turn north, and wind 10 miles through the army reservation to the oaks of your choice. At 12 miles, the Cone Peak Trail appears on the left; in another 2.5 miles, the Junipero Serra Peak climb starts on the right.

Muir Woods National Monument and Marin Headlands

LOCATION
north of San Francisco

LENGTH
1 mile or more

DIFFICULTY
easy to moderate

TREE SPECIES
redwoods, coast live oaks, Douglas firs

HIGHLIGHTS
largest redwood grove this far south, coast live oaks above the Pacific

The redwoods gain momentum in height and girth to the north, with groves in Henry Cowell and Big Basin Redwoods State Parks north of Santa Cruz, and then in a larger stand at Muir Woods National Monument north of San Francisco. This magnificent Marin County grove appears within a bus ride of America's fourth-largest urban area. The monument connects to adjoining state parks for a network of forest and grassland trails stretching northward.

Muir Woods National Monument is a 554-acre tract of old-growth redwoods along Redwood Creek and adjacent mountainsides a few miles from the ocean. While other redwood trails can be found along Big Sur's coast and the Santa Cruz Mountains south of San Francisco, the trees here are the largest south of the redwoods' primary range farther up the coast. Walk the Cathedral Grove Loop. Within a $3 bus ride from San Francisco, this and other Marin County trails wind among oaks, Douglas firs, and grasslands to the Marin Hills' highest peak, Mount Tamalpais, 2,580 feet immediately northward, and also northwest across rolling meadows to Stinson Beach, where Bay Area buses provide a return lift south after an all-day or multiday hike.

Winter here is good when it's not raining; springtime is lavishly green and flowered; summer is fine but sometimes foggy in the morning among the redwoods. Autumn is glorious, with grass that starts to green up after the first rains. Overall, Marin has some of the best year-round hiking trails in America, with no season presenting much in the way of limitations.

Expect a lot of company on weekends; the national monument, in particular, gets heavy traffic from tour buses. Reservations, available online through Muir Woods, are required for parking; make arrangements ahead of time or you'll be turned away. In that case, go to Muir Beach, 3 miles southwest, and walk back to the woods on a trail along Muir Woods Road—itself a pleasant stroll among alders if you're game for a longer trek.

Cross the Golden Gate Bridge northbound, go 5 miles on Highway 101, and exit on Highway 1

northbound. Wind uphill, turn right at the Muir Woods sign, and continue to the visitor center. Or stay on Highway 1 to Muir Beach's left turn, but instead go right 3 miles to the visitor center and redwood grove. See Golden Gate National Recreation Area maps for hikes in the crisscrossing network of Marin County trails.

OPPOSITE: Coast live oaks cluster along the ridges and slopes of Mount Tamalpais just north of Muir Woods.

Trails of the Marin Headlands and Golden Gate National Recreation Area west of Muir Woods lead to a medley of Douglas firs, coast live oaks, and windswept grasslands appearing in natural mosaics of vegetation, shown here at twilight while Pacific fog rolls in above Stinson Beach.

Humboldt Redwoods State Park

LOCATION
south of Eureka and Fortuna

LENGTH
short walks and up to 10 miles

DIFFICULTY
easy

TREE SPECIES
coast redwoods, Douglas firs, grand firs, western redcedars

HIGHLIGHTS
some of the tallest trees in the world

At Humboldt Redwoods State Park, a windblown redwood is not only a fallen tree, but also part of an ecosystem housing billions of invertebrates and microbes for hundreds of years to come.

OPPOSITE: Redwood trunks are home to entire ecosystems of mosses, lichens, and microbes integral to the greater functioning of the forest, catching water, providing nutrients, and catalyzing minerals and essential chemicals for the trees and creatures around them. Seething with life, this tree stands in the Bull Run Grove of the Humboldt Redwoods. A young tanoak—another critical player in the West Coast forest community— has taken root alongside.

Redwoods reach their prime here, up to 2,200 years old and growing taller than any other trees on earth, 380 feet at last count. These are among the purest cathedral-type stands of redwoods with nominal undergrowth.

The 53,000-acre park is one-third old growth and supports more extremely tall trees than anywhere else on earth. It also holds the world record for biomass—more living matter per acre than anywhere else. It's the largest single expanse of coast redwoods, with the largest riparian flats where deep soil and reliable water nourish the trees.

While this park and others may appear extensive to the casual visitor, only 5 percent of the ancient redwoods have survived logging. Big-tree aficionados, including Robert Van Pelt, believe that before the harvest of North Coast redwoods this species claimed not only the tallest, but also the largest trees on earth. Many redwoods were rescued from sawmill fates by the Save the Redwoods League, which has raised private funds to buy one grove after another since 1921, assembling a collective masterpiece that's still in progress and requiring more than a century to complete, not unlike the great cathedrals of Europe.

Sequestered along the South Fork Eel River, the Humboldt expanse of redwoods is unusual in being so far inland. This quirk of geography owes to distant southbound summer winds offshore creating ocean currents and turbulence that turns the

seawater over, exposing deep, cold marine water to surface air, which generates condensation of summertime fog. This gets blown inland and up the topographically welcoming Eel River Valley, where the year-round dampness is required by redwoods with their shallow roots and inability to tap deep groundwater sources. The region's Mediterranean climate lacks summer rainfall, but filling the gap, the ocean fog is blown against the tall redwoods' foliage, condenses in droplets, and drips to the ground in quantities totaling up to an incredible 30 inches annually. The redwoods' towering crowns have literally created their own climate—essential for the trees and serving the entire rainforest ecosystem. When too many tall trees are cut, the climate—and everything else—deteriorates.

Scenic Highway 101 runs 32 miles through the park and along the South Fork Eel. Watch for short trails marked with modest signs, for the visitor center at Myers Flat, and for favorite groves named Founders and Garden Club of America.

Some of the largest groves thrive along tributary Bull Creek, rated as the tallest canopy on the planet,

with 86 trees over 350 feet. Clear-cut logging farther upstream in industrial forests resulted in extreme erosion during floods of 1955 and 1964, when the creek undermined big trees. But most of the grove remained intact, and the Bull Creek Flats Trail loops 10 miles on both north and south sides of the stream. From Highway 101, north of Weott 2 miles, take the westbound turnoff and park on the west side of the South Fork Eel for the Bull Run Trail. Footbridges across the creek are erected for summer and fall only; hiking is otherwise limited to the north side or requires a deep ford ranging from sketchy to foolhardy in winter. Always doable, the half-mile Rockefeller Loop is a tantalizing introduction.

From San Francisco, drive north on Highway 101 past Garberville. Redwood trails begin north of Leggett with the mixed conifers of Standish-Hickey State Recreation Area, followed by Richardson Grove State Park, and then the greater wonders of Humboldt. North of Garberville, exit from Highway 101 onto Avenue of the Giants, a scenic route that reaches many trails and reconnects with the highway northward.

In Humboldt Redwoods State Park, the Bull Creek basin includes greater numbers of extremely tall trees than any other grove worldwide. The half-mile Rockefeller Loop makes a good introduction to a longer trek, just west of the South Fork Eel River and near the Avenue of the Giants scenic highway.

Prairie Creek Redwoods State Park

For height, size, and total rainforest community, my favorite redwood groves are at Prairie Creek.

Like Humboldt, Prairie Creek Redwoods State Park includes some of the world's tallest trees. Of the 20 largest redwoods reported in 2001 by Robert Van Pelt in *Forest Giants of the Pacific Coast*, 15 appear here. Being farther from the main highway, and with extensive backcountry and uninterrupted wild acreage through much of its 14,000 acres, this park is exceptional. Prairie Creek differs from the Humboldt groves in ecological makeup; closer to the ocean, this rain forest includes western hemlocks and Sitka spruces—the world's largest spruce species, including a 300-foot giant.

Seventy-five miles of trails provide for strolls and hikes. From the visitor center, walk northward ascending Prairie Creek and its tributaries. Longer routes link to the ocean. With reservations, walk-in campsites make a two- or three-day adventure through redwoods possible here like nowhere else; backpack camping is typically not allowed in other redwood parks.

Related attractions are Roosevelt elk, frequently seen at Elk Prairie near the visitor center or Gold Bluffs Beach, which is reached via a gravel road or the James Irvine Trail—7 miles one way including Fern Canyon, a rock-walled gorge totally bedecked in ferns near the sea. An easy car shuttle takes you back or, better, connect with the Ossagon Trail for a 15-mile car-free loop. An alternate 11-mile loop from the visitor center also reaches the Pacific Ocean via the James Irvine and Miner's Ridge Trails.

Prairie Creek makes for a remarkable experience all year. Winter can be rainy, cool, and damp, but those months show the essence of the rain forest, and a sweater, raincoat, and umbrella are

LOCATION
north of Arcata and Orick

LENGTH
1 to 15 miles

DIFFICULTY
easy to moderate

TREE SPECIES
coast redwoods, bigleaf maples

HIGHLIGHTS
some of the finest redwoods, remote groves

Roosevelt elk are the largest species of elk and often appear in Prairie Creek Redwoods State Park. To see them, ask at the visitor center, watch in the meadow there, or consider a drive on gravel roads to Gold Bluffs Beach.

adequate keys to comfort, at least for day hikes. Spring is as full of life as the Appalachians. Summer is pleasantly temperate, if not cool, when thermometers inland top 100 degrees. Fog may shroud the mornings, but skies typically clear by noon. Watch for utterly magical moments when the sun begins to burn through fog at the crowns of the 300-foot trees and shine down in distinct rays of light between the branches at, say, 10:00 a.m. Fall is colorful, with willows and maples aglow and sweet weather that can linger through November.

From Arcata, drive Highway 101 north 40 miles. Just beyond Orick, exit onto the Newton B. Drury Scenic Parkway, and soon go left to the visitor center. Trails leave from there and also from pullouts along the parkway running northbound 10 miles before reconnecting with Highway 101.

In another 12 miles northward, Highway 101 bisects Del Norte Coast Redwoods State Park—less showy and accessible but with its own redwoods and a path through Damnation Creek Grove. Drive north of the Klamath River, pass the Wilson Creek Beach, and continue uphill to milepost 16, with a small sign and modest west-side parking area. The path immediately enters an impressive grove, then crosses the Coast Range to steep slopes veering down to Pacific breakers.

Rhododendrons bloom from late May to mid-June at Pacific coast redwood groves. Here, at Del Norte Coast Redwoods State Park, 10 miles south of Crescent City, a trail off Highway 101 tours this grove and continues westward to bluffs above the Pacific Ocean.

Jedediah Smith Redwoods State Park

LOCATION
east of Crescent City

LENGTH
0.5 to 6 miles, loops or out and back

DIFFICULTY
easy to moderate

TREE SPECIES
coast redwoods, bigleaf maples, vine maples

HIGHLIGHTS
redwoods and mixed conifers, California's most pristine large river

This park straddles the Smith River—California's largest undammed stream and finest salmon waters—where woodland trails parallel and finger up from the banks. Classic, the Stout Grove of giant redwoods occupies the river's fertile floodplain, which means this grove is virtually flat, making it possible to see literally 100 large trees in a single rotation of view.

The grove's shortest approach in summer is from the state park campground; from the main entrance, drive to the end of the campground, park, walk to the gravel beach, cross a seasonal footbridge over the Smith, cross Mill Creek's boardwalk, and stroll the half-mile ancient grove loop. In all other seasons, when the Smith River footbridge is not available, drive east to Highway 199's commercial cluster of Hiouchi. In another mile, turn right on South Fork Road, bridge the Middle and then South Fork of the Smith, stay right, and proceed on gravel to Stout Grove on the right.

Other trails wind along Mill Creek and follow the Smith's southern shore downstream from Stout Grove—20 miles altogether. Jedediah Smith, Prairie Creek, and Del Norte Redwoods State Parks are comanaged with nearby federal land as Redwood National and State Parks. Stop at the visitor center along Highway 199 west of Hiouchi.

Redwoods are majestic any time of year. Summer is delightfully mild here when California's interior bakes. In winter, the Smith floods with some of the heaviest downpours on the West Coast—an amazing sight and hydrologic phenomena if you don't mind braving rain that's usually still falling when the river crests.

From Crescent City, drive north on Highway 101 and exit on Highway 199 east. Enter the park, cross the Smith River, and continue to the entrance and

The Stout Grove in Jedediah Smith Redwoods State Park towers as one of the finest cathedral-type redwood forests—a pure stand on the floodplain of the Smith River.

Delicate starry leaves of a vine maple catch sunlight penetrating a thin opening skyward at the Stout Grove. Native Americans of the Pacific coast wove the supple, multiple stems of this "basket tree" into vessels for carrying clams, fish, and other food.

OPPOSITE: Redwood trunks at the Stout Grove disappear into the sky above; the treetops can rarely be seen except at a distance.

campground on the right, 9 miles from Crescent City. For the visitor center, go slightly farther east on Route 199 and turn left at the sign.

This is the northernmost cathedral-like grove of redwoods, but two more stands appear in Oregon: the obscure Winchuck Forest and the more accessible Chetco Grove. Drive north on Highway 101. Before downtown Brookings, turn right on North Bank Chetco River Road and go 7 miles. Beyond Alfred A. Loeb State Park's campground, watch for the small left-side pullout.

PACIFIC NORTHWEST

Legendary for trees, the Pacific Northwest is home to Douglas firs, grand firs, western redcedars, hemlocks, and others that make up some of the most extensive large conifer forests on earth, not to mention bigleaf maples, black cottonwoods, and Oregon white oaks. Sitka spruces stand along the Pacific as stormy-shore giants matching, in arboreal scale, the grandeur of the ocean itself. And trails in this region are among the best.

At the south coast of Oregon, the Siskiyou Mountains—combined seamlessly with the Klamath Mountains of Northern California—bridge vast terrain between the north-south lineup of the combined Sierra Nevada and Cascade Mountains that rise 100 miles inland and the paralleling Coast Range edging the Pacific Ocean. The Klamath-Siskiyou Mountains nourish America's top variety of conifers—33 species—the regional equivalent of the Appalachians' biologically endowed Smoky Mountains.

Much of the Coast Range within 50 miles of the Pacific is in timber-industry ownership, and almost all of it has been logged, then logged again. A few gems endure: the Elk River basin's national forest wilderness in southern Oregon remains an island of old growth surrounded by seas of clear-cuts, and the Drift Creek and Cummins Creek Wildernesses of ancient trees lie at the state's central coast. Smaller exquisite groves draw us to state parks along Oregon's Pacific shores.

Inland 100 miles, the Cascade Range of volcanic peaks roughen the skyline of Oregon and Washington with snowcapped summits as symmetrical as those drawn by a first grader. Though far more woodlands have been protected here than in the cutover Coast Range, fewer than one in 10 acres are safeguarded as wilderness. Yet these offer whole Edens of ancient firs, hemlocks, and cedars. East of there, freestanding mountain ranges across drylands of the two states give rise to terrestrial islands of forest surrounded by steppes, deserts, and gorges as deep as Hells Canyon of the Snake River.

Northward, the Olympic Mountains of Washington take rain forests to a whole new level with record sizes of firs, cedars, and hemlocks. Olympic National Park is an American paragon for wild forests, with memorable trails up the Queets, Quinault, and Hoh Rivers. Like an entire empire, and beyond reach for most of us, Alaska lies farther north.

The Pacific Northwest was the epicenter of modern movements to protect forests; an awakening in the 1980s recognized that only a precious 10 percent of public-land old growth in the Cascade Mountains remained. Nationwide, only a few percent of the original forest remained intact—if that—with virtually none in many states. Recognizing this fact, and also the ecological shortcomings of management for cutover land, spirited campaigns were launched to save as much as possible of what remained and to improve forest practices. This led to the Clinton Administration's Northwest Forest Plan of 1994, which set aside most of the scarce ancient federal forest that persisted west of the Cascade Crest and established nominal no-cut buffers along streams. Timber interests repeatedly tried to rescind even these limited safeguards with continuing threats—in spite of the industry holding a sharply shrinking piece of the economic pie, down from highs in the 1950s to only one percent of Oregon's jobs today, losses owing principally to automation and log exports.

Increasing wildfires—"climate" fires, really—are driven by the droughts and winds of global warming and have led not only to excruciating losses and suffering but also to rancorous discourse and political struggle here and throughout the West. The timber industry claims that more logging is necessary to reduce the fuel (i.e., cut the trees so they won't burn). But forest advocates point out that the crowded plantation thickets growing in the wake of clear-cut logging are the most flammable of all and a central source of the problem. Furthermore, mature trees—with their thick asbestos-like bark and long, limbless boles lifting the green crowns high above the lick of flames—effectively cast deep shade, conserve moisture, and maintain cooler temperatures, all meaning that old forests are the least likely to burn intensely. Restoring old-growth characteristics is the best forest-management prescription for fire protection.

Meanwhile, for the hiker, public land of the Pacific Northwest awaits with wooded paths threading up the valleys and mountains. Crater Lake, Olympic, and North Cascades National Parks all highlight alluring

possibilities, while 12 national forests link along the Cascade Crest. No less tempting, 57 of Oregon's state parks and others in Washington enchant with beach strolls and vigorous climbs to Pacific headlands.

Hikers prepared for rain enjoy coastal trails all winter, as well as low-elevation Cascade Mountain trails, which rise to snow levels and are the province of cross-country skiers until springtime's melt. Summers are dry and clear, and autumn is excellent throughout.

We'll first migrate up the coast of Oregon, then tour the state's Cascade Range from south to north, then explore the forests of Washington, and finally make a stop in the wilds of Alaska.

Coquille River Falls,
Rogue River-Siskiyou National Forest

OREGON

LOCATION
southwest Oregon, south of
Coquille and Powers

LENGTH
1-mile out and back

DIFFICULTY
strenuous

TREE SPECIES
Douglas firs, western
hemlocks, bigleaf maples,
Port Orford cedars

HIGHLIGHTS
old-growth conifers, waterfall

PREVIOUS SPREAD: Thriving on ocean air rich with the magnesium of salt spray, Sitka spruces are the reigning conifer at the Pacific edge in Oregon and northward across southern Alaska to Kodiak Island. These spruces enchant at Port Orford Heads State Park.

Enveloped in the green of bigleaf maples and alders, Coquille River Falls culminates in this pocket of sunshine after a half-mile walk through spectacular old-growth firs, cedars, and hemlocks.

OPPOSITE: East of Coquille River Falls, the trail up Mount Bolivar summits with views to recent burns but also to old-growth conifers on cooler northern slopes and in deep ravines.

A steep trail down to the South Fork Coquille River winds among giant conifers the whole way, ending at a fabulously ornate waterfall—three, actually, in one grand view.

This out-of-the-way elevation in the Siskiyou Mountains is snow-free all winter, but spring is exhilarating when the river runs strong and the fresh greens of bigleaf maples and carpets of ground covers overwhelm the senses. From Powers, drive south 18 miles on Forest Road 33, turn left on Forest Road 3348, and go 1.5 miles to the falls' left-side pullout.

While nearby, stop at the California bay (myrtle) trees in Hoffman Memorial State Wayside south of Myrtle Point. And also visit the largest Port Orford cedar, thus far discordantly surviving among clear-cuts. Six miles south of Powers, turn left on Forest Road 3358 and go 4 miles to the sign on the right.

Beyond Coquille River Falls, continue on Forest Road 3348 eastbound 8 miles, turn right on dirt Forest Road 5520, and then left on Forest Road 230 to Hanging Rock trailhead. Climb 2 miles to the thrilling outcrop and continue westward along Panther Ridge for old growth. Back on paved Forest Road 3348, drive another 9 miles east for the steep climb to Mount Bolivar, whose trail tours the green-up of forest succession following a 2005 fire, including fire-dependent knobcone pines and surviving ancient trees on cooler north-facing slopes, before it tops out on one of the Siskiyou Mountains' sharpest peaks.

Big Tree Trail, Oregon Caves National Monument and Preserve

OREGON

LOCATION
east of Cave Junction

LENGTH
4-mile loop

DIFFICULTY
moderate to strenuous

TREE SPECIES
Douglas firs, canyon live oaks, tanoaks, bigleaf maples, Port Orford cedars, incense cedars, madrones, sugar pines, white firs

HIGHLIGHTS
largest Douglas fir in Oregon, diversity of Northwest trees

This hike with 1,100 feet of elevation gain is found at Oregon Caves National Monument and Preserve, administered by the National Park Service and the next best thing Oregon has to a second national park (Crater Lake is the only one).

Start behind the visitor center on the Cliff Nature Trail, and in a mile bear right on the Big Tree Trail loop. The destination is Oregon's largest Douglas fir (this name is often spelled Douglas-fir, with the hyphen intended to indicate that the tree is taxonomically not a true fir). The age of the 14-foot-diameter methuselah is estimated at 1,000 years. It's a reminder that, according to big-tree chronicler Robert Van Pelt, the tallest tree ever known was not a coast redwood, but a Douglas fir whose remains near Mount Rainier in Washington were measured in the early 1900s at 393 feet.

Watch also for Port Orford cedars—stately conifers endemic mainly to the Oregon coast and centered on the town of Port Orford. To consider the biological perils of globalism, look no further: nearly all the old Port Orford cedars were logged for export to Japan, where they were coveted because that country's similar Hinoki cypress had been recklessly cut to virtual extinction. Meanwhile, nursery stock infected with a deadly fungus-like pathogen, *Phytophthora lateralis*, was imported from Asia to the Northwest. Mobilized by water, including mud stuck in tires of log trucks pounding thousands of miles of remote roads, the disease spread widely and killed nearly all the remaining Port Orford cedars. Five percent tend to be resistant, and seeds from those have been cultivated in nursery stock for outplanting to recolonize the exceptional tree. I've got them growing in my own backyard in—yes—Port Orford! (The tree was named for the town, though of course the tree came first.)

Oregon Caves is open all year, but winter rain, chill, and snow can be formidable. Spring, summer, and fall are good times to visit.

Drive to the town of Cave Junction on Highway 199 north of the California line, turn east on Route 46/Oregon Caves Highway, and go 20 miles.

The largest (though not tallest) Douglas fir in Oregon stands along the Big Tree Trail in Oregon Caves National Monument and Preserve. Historic records indicate that Douglas firs once exceeded 400 feet in height and ranked as the tallest trees in the world.

OPPOSITE: The wheel-like foliage of vanilla leaf shares the ground with Oregon grape and twisted stalk at Oregon Caves. Like many other broadleaf plants in the shaded forests of the Pacific Northwest, vanilla leaf flattens upward to the sky in order to catch light efficiently.

Humbug Mountain State Park

OREGON

LOCATION
north of Gold Beach

LENGTH
5-mile loop

DIFFICULTY
strenuous

TREE SPECIES
Douglas firs, western hemlocks, bigleaf maples, California bays

HIGHLIGHTS
old-growth trail to a Coast Range summit

Humbug Mountain, 1,756 feet, is the tallest peak rising directly out of the ocean along Oregon's coast, and this trail switchbacks to its top while passing through impressive old growth—a stellar forest hike that's also a mountain hike and workout.

According to local Native Americans, Humbug was more descriptively called "thok'eh-meep'ush" (various spellings), meaning "salmon cheek," because the triangular rise of this landmark resembles the shape of the muscle at the cheek of a salmon.

The Humbug Mountain Trail begins in a resinous grove of towering California bays, locally known as myrtles. The path climbs and in a mile branches into a loop, the right side being shorter and sunnier to the summit. Both options include old-growth Douglas firs up to five feet across, plus bigleaf maples, large western hemlocks, and grand firs, which, like hemlocks, tolerate shade.

State park foresters clear-cut the mountaintop's south-facing slope to reopen a historic view. They badly overdid it by chainsawing mature trees that were essential as a windbreak for rare old growth directly behind, which predictably blew down with the first storm, leaving at the summit forest a powerline-like gap that's visible for 10 miles north and south. The rest of the trail remains one of the longest Coast Range paths through ancient forest.

From Gold Beach, drive north on Highway 101 for 24 miles. Beyond the campground, turn left at the sign.

A rare coastal snowstorm whitens Douglas firs at Humbug Mountain's summit.

Ancient trees wracked by winter
windstorms survive near the top
of Humbug Mountain.

Port Orford Heads State Park

This state park along Oregon's coast has a loop trail with magnificent Sitka spruces and wind-sculpted pines within an elegant mosaic of deep forests, open meadows, coastal scrub, and rocky headlands.

From the parking lot and its nearby lawn, find three trails—Cove, Tower, and Headland. All begin in groves of big-limbed Sitka spruces. The Cove Trail departs clockwise around the perimeter of the park with views southward to Humbug Mountain, then to ocean panoramas. Being on a peninsula, the trail's southern apex affords a rare opportunity to look across a breadth of ocean and see the forested (and industrially clear-cut) West Coast on the other side rather than only water. At an overlook farther west, seals often appear below, and whales pass through.

Wind factors in here, with a steady blow from the north in the sunny summer and fearsome storms from the south in the winter, all shaping exposed trees into distinctive wind-contoured sculptures like those normally seen only with alpine krummholz.

Winter storms from November to April can bring drenching rains and shrieking winds, but between storms hiking here, and elsewhere on Oregon's coast, is possible when higher mountains to the east lie snowbound. Summer stays cool when the interior broils.

From Highway 101 in Port Orford, turn west on 9th Street, drive two blocks, bear left, and climb to the parking lot.

OREGON

LOCATION
south of Bandon, at Port Orford

LENGTH
2-mile loop

DIFFICULTY
easy

TREE SPECIES
Sitka spruces, shore pines, grand firs

HIGHLIGHTS
Sitka spruce forest, wind-sculpted shore pines

The loop trail at Port Orford Heads State Park begins and ends in magnificent groves of Sitka spruce—America's fourth-tallest tree, in some places exceeding 250 feet.

Cape Blanco State Park

LOCATION
north of Port Orford, south of Bandon

LENGTH
3 miles

DIFFICULTY
easy to moderate

TREE SPECIES
Sitka spruces, shore pines

HIGHLIGHTS
wind-sculpted spruce forest, driftwood

A forest tour of the West could arguably end here, as Cape Blanco is the westernmost point in the contiguous states except for the tip of Washington. At this narrow peninsula winds are some of the strongest and most constant on the coast, shaping trees and forests in artistic ways. Only grass, wildflowers, and coastal scrub can take the full brunt, but with the slightest shelter, Sitka spruces and shore pines (a subspecies of lodgepole) begin as krummholz dwarfed by wind pruning. Desiccated branches provide shelter for leeward shoots that grow progressively larger downwind until the trees become massive.

For a 3-mile hike, drive to the end of the road toward the lighthouse, walk back 100 yards to a path mowed into coastal scrub, and head north. This path morphs from meadow to picturesque wind-sculpted forest edge, then on to larger Sitka spruces and an eerily thick forest tunneled by the trail. Stay left and descend toward the Sixes River and its spectacular mouth among offshore crags, where seals, shorebirds, and eagles might all be seen.

Appreciate the monumental piles of driftwood—a forest in yet another form that has accumulated after the trees fell into rivers, floated to sea, and returned on storm surges. Loop back south via the beach to your car.

Winter brings prohibitive storms that blow from the south up to 100 miles per hour, with horizontal rain sometimes dropping five inches at a clip. But in between these extreme low-pressure events the weather can be intoxicatingly mild, so watch the forecast. Spring, summer, and fall are good, but often cool and foggy, and expect a stiff wind from the north in summer.

From Port Orford, take Highway 101 north 7 miles, turn west at the Cape Blanco sign, and go to the end.

At Cape Blanco State Park, Sitka spruces grow thick, with annual rainfall of a hundred inches or more on slopes veering down to the Pacific, while sword ferns grow as ground cover.

OPPOSITE: The legacy of northwestern forests lives on even after riverfront trees have fallen, floated downstream, flushed to sea, and washed back ashore. Logs here, at the northern end of Cape Blanco State Park, create a whole landscape and ecosystem on the beach near the Sixes River mouth. Sitka spruces green the background.

Marys Peak,
Siuslaw National Forest

OREGON

LOCATION
west of Corvallis

LENGTH
1 to 5 miles out and back
or loop

DIFFICULTY
easy to moderate

TREE SPECIES
Douglas firs, noble firs,
western redcedars, western
hemlocks

HIGHLIGHTS
Coast Range mountaintop
forest

Marys Peak, 4,098 feet high and 25 miles from the ocean, is the highest summit in the Oregon Coast Range, and a paved road provides access to a rare coastal forest that has not been thoroughly logged.

Hiking is inviting all year, with occasional winter snow. Even in rain from November to May, forests are beautifully eerie in green-to-gray gradations as moisture increases with distance—an atmosphere of wildness just one step off the road.

For the full view, and interludes of old-growth conifers, take the 5-mile loop using the Summit Loop, North Ridge, Tie, and East Ridge Trails.

From Corvallis, drive west on Route 34 for 14 miles and watch closely on the right for Marys Peak Road. Stay right on Forest Road 3010 to the Observation Point parking lot, and then see the trail map.

Near the summit of Marys Peak, lichens cloak the trunks of grand firs like fur and a winter rainstorm saturates the limbs of a young western hemlock—excelling in shade where other trees cannot.

Cape Lookout State Park

OREGON

LOCATION
southwest of Tillamook

LENGTH
5 miles out and back

DIFFICULTY
moderate

TREE SPECIES
Sitka spruces, western
hemlocks

HIGHLIGHTS
oceanfront Sitka spruce
forest

Sitka spruces define the natural art of Oregon's coast, and Cape Lookout is a gallery of trees on a prowl of rock jutting into the Pacific Ocean with dramatic cliffs, seaward views, and severe weather.

The Cape Lookout Trail runs 2.5 miles to the ultimate outpost. Also starting from the parking lot, the North Trail immediately enters its own ancient Sitka and hemlock grove. This overlaps with the state-length Oregon Coast Trail of 362 miles, some of it outstanding, though major sections remain relegated to the Highway 101 shoulder.

The cape is scenic all year, with its raw, wet, wind-driven character evident through winter. The Mediterranean climate means virtually no rain in summer and persistent cool winds no matter how hot it gets inland.

From Tillamook, on Highway 101 turn west on 3rd Street toward Three Capes and drive 13 miles to the trailhead.

Similar, Cape Meares State Scenic Viewpoint lies 18 miles farther north and has trails and Sitka spruces of its own, including the bizarre Octopus Tree on a bluff overlooking the ocean, plus a Sitka spruce ranked as the third-largest tree in Oregon.

The Cape Lookout Trail runs 2.5 miles
through Sitka spruces dampened
by rainstorms, fog, and walls of
windblown mist from the Pacific.

Sitka spruces tower overhead and cast their own twilight of shade at Cape Lookout State Park.

OPPOSITE: Jutting boldly into the Pacific Ocean, Cape Lookout ends with Sitka spruces dwarfed by wind and a thicket of green salal at the edge of the continent.

Crater Lake National Park

Oregon's only national park is famous for its name-sake: the 6-mile-wide caved-in caldera remaining after Mount Mazama's eruption 7,700 years ago—now the deepest, bluest lake in America. A conifer forest encircles that gem, and the Rim Drive and Rim Trail provide easy access.

Never logged, weathered by fearsome storms, and backdropped by dazzling views, the forests along the caldera rim are wildly photogenic. While western hemlocks occupy many of the Cascade and Coast Range forests at lower elevations, mountain hemlocks—which John Muir in 1894 called "the most singularly beautiful" of conifers—grow at higher levels and reach impressive girth. Here, they steal the show with dark-green needle masses, wind-sculpted branches, and nodding crowns and limbs that bend to drop their snow load rather than supporting it by brute strength. After dying, these and whitebark pines weather to bleached white limbs pounded by harsh winter storms around the caldera's rim.

Park at Crater Lake Lodge and walk westward on the Rim Trail with liberties to wander and admire eye-catching trees of the centuries. The overlook of Wizard Island is one of many intriguing sites.

The trail continues 33 miles, weaving back and forth across the road with views not only to the lake but also to Cascade ridges; California's distant snow cone, Mount Shasta; and the glacier-reduced Mount Thielsen to the north, its craggy core electrically hardened by lightning through the ages. A short walk east from the comforts of Crater Lake Lodge climbs Mount Garfield with its own suite of weathered trees.

Summer is nice here, with a cool breeze at high elevations. In winter, the Park Service plows the road to the rim—but not around it—making this

OREGON

LOCATION
northeast of Medford

LENGTH
1 to 33 miles

DIFFICULTY
easy to strenuous

TREE SPECIES
mountain hemlocks,
whitebark pines

HIGHLIGHTS
mountain hemlock groves,
lake views

Mountain hemlocks reach their prime at the rim of the Crater Lake caldera in the southern Cascade Mountains. Unlike trees that accommodate the weight of snow and the force of wind through muscular limbs and superior strength, hemlocks respond with a special talent to flex. The nodding tops and weeping branches droop, shed their snow load, and spring back to absorb the winter sun. Mountain hemlocks occupy some of the snowiest forest zones of North America.

Mountain hemlocks cluster in groves between the deepest snowbanks near the Crater Lake rim.

OPPOSITE: Along with artistic forms of mountain hemlocks, whitebark pines at Crater Lake's caldera assume sculptural forms in ancient remains of trees that died decades ago. Unfortunately, an exotic fungus, *Cronartium ribicola*, is killing a large portion of the whitebarks and other members of the white pine family nationwide. These pines grow under the harshest high-elevation conditions and are a critical food source for at least 13 bird and eight mammal species across the West, including grizzly and black bears.

a place to ski or snowshoe in terrain thoroughly whitened through June. Late-spring consolidation makes for easy snow-top walking without breaking through. Autumn is glorious.

From I-5 at Medford, take Highway 62 north. In 70 miles, turn left at the Crater Lake sign, stay left at the Rim Drive intersection, ascend to the top, and go right to the parking lot.

North Umpqua Trail, Umpqua National Forest

This trail runs 79 miles in 12 segments of 4 to 16 miles each, which can be done as day hikes or backpack outings following a scenic river to headwaters at 6,000-foot Maidu Lake, where another path connects to the Pacific Crest Trail. Avoid poison oak along the lower 10 miles. As elevation increases, forests transform to white firs, Shasta red firs, lodgepole pines, western white pines, and mountain hemlocks.

At the bottom, the Swiftwater Trailhead is reached quickly from a major paved road not far off I-5, leading hikers to ancient forests with firs up to six feet in diameter. A 2-mile out and back is usually snow-free in winter. A short spur trail near the outset leads to Deadline Falls of the North Umpqua River, where salmon and steelhead can occasionally be seen jumping from May to October.

Similar Oregon trails follow other Cascade Mountain rivers—the upper Rogue to the south, and the Middle Fork Willamette, McKenzie, Clackamas, and Salmon to the north. All are worthwhile, but this North Umpqua route is the longest and best for extended backpacking.

From I-5 at Roseburg, drive east on Route 138 past Idleyd Park. At 22 miles from Roseburg, turn right toward Swiftwater Park/Deadline Falls, cross the bridge, and turn left.

OREGON

LOCATION
east of Roseburg

LENGTH
1 mile or more out and back, up to 79 miles one way

DIFFICULTY
easy to strenuous

TREE SPECIES
Douglas firs, western hemlocks, bigleaf maples, sugar pines

HIGHLIGHTS
old-growth conifers, river frontage

At the lower end of the North Umpqua Trail, Douglas firs have made stately columns for centuries. In the shaded understory, the ubiquitous northwestern shrub salal thickens in dark green, poison oak grows robustly at the far right, and Oregon grape clings to the ground. This trail continues 79 miles to Cascade Mountain highcountry.

Constitution Grove, Willamette National Forest

OREGON

LOCATION
northeast of Oakridge

LENGTH
1 mile

DIFFICULTY
easy

TREE SPECIES
Douglas firs, western redcedars, western hemlocks

HIGHLIGHTS
old-growth Douglas firs

This easy stroll is immersed in one of the finest Douglas fir and west-slope Cascade Mountain forests of ancient trees, some 400 years old.

Cascade forests have been clear-cut throughout much of the range, and fires have increased with the droughts and winds of global warming, but this unlogged grove in Willamette National Forest remains a refuge. Bordering the North Fork of the Middle Fork Willamette River, the path loops among conifers with elegant vine maples and maidenhair ferns.

Spring through fall is beautiful here, and, even though this grove sits deep within folds of the Cascade Mountains, the snow level is usually higher during rainy winters.

From Eugene, take Route 58 southeast. Four miles before Oakridge, at the sign for Westfir, turn left and cross the Middle Fork Willamette. Turn left to Westfir, and follow Forest Road 19/Aufderheide Drive up the North Fork 27 paved miles.

Dripping with groundwater and a rain-soaked forest floor at the Constitution Grove in Willamette National Forest, maidenhair ferns with articulated fronds thrive, along with twisted stalk in parallel veins and coltsfoot with trilobed leaves flattened to the light.

McKenzie River Trail, Willamette National Forest

OREGON

LOCATION
east of Eugene

LENGTH
26 miles, shorter day trips

DIFFICULTY
easy to moderate

TREE SPECIES
western hemlocks, Douglas firs, western redcedars

HIGHLIGHTS
old-growth riparian forest, waterfalls, logjams

Downstream from Deer Creek, the McKenzie River Trail tours one of the finer old-growth groves in the state.

FOLLOWING SPREAD: The McKenzie River rushes with steep gradient in the shade of western hemlocks and green splays of western redcedars.

This is one of the finest riverfront old-growth trails in the West, with tall crowns casting shade and large fallen trees providing aquatic habitat and an extended tour of the forest-river interface. Cutting through the valley, Highway 126 is sometimes heard but rarely seen from the trail.

The hike is easily broken into day trips or backpacking outings. Starting at the upper end, the McKenzie River's source lies near Clear Lake, formed by a lava dam 3,000 years ago. From a canoe on the crystalline waters, the remains of standing trees can still be seen preserved in the cold anaerobic medium of the lake. The trunks are not large, but they're the oldest standing dead trees one is ever likely to see except for bristlecone pines.

Downriver, the trail skirts the enthralling 120-foot Sahalie Falls, followed by 90-foot Koosah Falls and a primeval canyon packed with big trees and logjams forming sieves of turbulent rapids. A 2-mile loop makes a terrific short hike. After interruption by a hydropower dam downstream, the trail resumes through another splendid old-growth section both above and below the Deer Creek Trailhead. See especially the old growth half a mile downstream from the creek.

Summer is outstanding here, when the spring-fed river ranks among the coldest in the state. Fall is bright with bigleaf and vine maples.

From Eugene, drive east on Highway 126 to trailheads starting near the Willamette National Forest ranger station east of McKenzie Bridge. Park also at Deer Creek, Trail Bridge Reservoir, and Sahalie Falls, which is often crowded.

Wallace Marine Park

This walk passes through a deciduous floodplain forest of cottonwoods, a keystone species on which many others—including owls, songbirds, and small mammals—depend. The park also shows how woodland thickets act as filtering systems for nearby runoff and for floods that seasonally saturate the valley.

The 114-acre park is principally used for its athletic fields, and at my last visit the tents of a few homeless campers were hidden in the woods, but this cottonwood forest is among the best along the 187-mile-long Willamette River.

Walking here is good most of the time, but winter's high water can mean soggy ground. Fall—when the cottonwood grove becomes a palace of yellow and gold, each leaf a masterpiece of painted foliage, and the scent of autumn sweetens the air—is brilliant.

From downtown Salem, take Highway 22 to the west side of the Willamette River, turn right on Route 221, drive north through the commercial strip half a mile, and watch for the Wallace Marine Park sign on the right. From the parking lot, walk toward the river to paths leading upstream half a mile.

Other cottonwood groves fill forested parklands along the Willamette at Eugene, Corvallis, Albany, Salem, and Willamette Mission State Park, where the world's largest black cottonwood can be found along with big black walnut trees.

Like an intermediate sky, the crowns of black cottonwoods dome overhead on a crisp autumn day at Wallace Marine Park.

OPPOSITE: In one of many urban riverfront forests along the Willamette River, black cottonwoods rise high at Wallace Marine Park in the city of Salem. Exotic and invasive English ivy encroaches on trunks at the bottom; local volunteer weed pullers are needed here and wherever the invasive ivy is found.

LaPine State Park

OREGON

LOCATION
southwest of Bend

LENGTH
1-mile out and back

DIFFICULTY
easy

TREE SPECIES
ponderosa pines

HIGHLIGHTS
largest ponderosa pine in Oregon

Ponderosas are the widest-ranging pines in North America, from British Columbia southward into Mexico and the Pacific coast to central Nebraska, 15 large states in all. Some trees reach 227 feet.

This short, paved walk in LaPine State Park leads to one of the fattest ponderosas, 9.1 feet in diameter and 168 feet tall in 2013, estimated at 500 years old.

In the semidry forest buffering the lush Cascade Crest to the west from the desert steppe eastward, fire-resistant trees like this one historically typified ponderosa forests growing among grasslands that burned frequently following summertime lightning strikes. The large pines resisted damage with thick, asbestos-like bark as suits of armor, limbless boles, and clear understories frequently tidied up by small fires. But then virtually all the large trees were cut, and the small lightning fires were suppressed, leading to a thicker, crowded forest of stunted trees packed with resinous new growth and prone to larger, hotter, uncontrollable fires. The great pine here is a reminder of the scale of fire-resistant trees once common before they were cut down across western woodlands.

In some areas, the Forest Service and Bureau of Land Management thin and then periodically burn the crowded understory with controlled fires, leaving larger trees amid grasslands, as seen in the nearby Deschutes National Forest on roads to Bachelor Butte and Sisters.

From the parking lot, take the paved trail north toward the Deschutes River. A footpath continues upstream along the water, leading to a few other mature pines and a recovering forest.

From La Pine (30 miles south of Bend), drive north on Highway 97 for 6 miles, turn west toward LaPine State Park, go 4 miles, turn right toward the campground, and then turn right to the parking lot.

A giant ponderosa pine leans toward sunlight along the Deschutes River while a forest of lodgepole pines crowd nearby.

OPPOSITE: At LaPine State Park, this ponderosa pine is the largest in the state and reportedly the greatest in circumference worldwide. A short, paved walk leads to the base of the monumental tree, and paths continue through a waterfront forest along the Deschutes River.

Metolius River, Deschutes National Forest

OREGON

LOCATION
northwest of Bend, west of Sisters

LENGTH
2 miles out and back or more

DIFFICULTY
easy

TREE SPECIES
ponderosa pines, Douglas firs, incense cedars

HIGHLIGHTS
riverfront ponderosa pines

At one of the more exquisite ponderosa groves of the interior West, gold-plated trunks rise along the Metolius River, reached by paths downstream from Camp Sherman.

Crystal-clear waters of the Metolius River emerge full-sized from a spring beneath Mount Jefferson and flow north with a paved road alongside that passes 12 campgrounds. Take a walk of any length on trails that line both sides of the stream.

Ponderosa pines are elegant here, with their thick golden trunks, ground cover of grass and wildflowers, and open understory. The Forest Service has managed controlled burns to reestablish a fire-tolerant ecosystem like what was once typical of dry pinelands east of the Cascade Crest before all the largest trees were cut down.

Go to the lower (northeast) end of the river road, park at Lower Bridge, and walk upstream on the west side. Continuous with this trail, or as a separate day hike, walk upstream from the Wizard Falls Fish Hatchery parking lot to Canyon Creek Campground, passing pine groves, whitewater, and bubbling springs that add appreciably to the river's volume.

From Bend, drive northwest on Highway 20 to Sisters, then go another 9 miles. Turn right on Camp Sherman Road/Forest Road 14, select a pullout or campground connecting to riverfront trails, or continue 15 miles to Lower Bridge.

Much farther east in Oregon, fine ponderosa groves and savannas can also be found along the Imnaha River south of Joseph. At the equally remote Malheur and North Malheur Rivers, riverfront trails tour ponderosa stands. More typically found in the Northern Rockies of Idaho and Montana, western larches also thrive along the Malheur, growing arrow straight and six feet in diameter.

Clackamas River, Mount Hood National Forest

OREGON

LOCATION
southeast of Portland

LENGTH
2 to 8 miles out and back

DIFFICULTY
easy to moderate

TREE SPECIES
Douglas firs, western hemlocks, western redcedars, white alders

HIGHLIGHTS
old-growth conifers

Ancient Douglas firs crown the trail along the Clackamas River in the Cascade Mountains. The trail from Rainbow Campground to Riverside Campground appeals to hikers from spring through fall.

OPPOSITE: The 1-mile trail to Alder Flat on the Clackamas River passes through ancient forest the whole way. Douglas firs, western hemlocks, and western redcedars yield to a picturesque grove of alders at the riverfront.

Two sections of trail along the Clackamas River rank among the finest old-growth hikes in the Portland area and statewide. Both tread through shaded corridors of Douglas firs, western hemlocks, western redcedars, and bigleaf maples.

From I-205 south of Portland, take exit 12/Clackamas, follow Highway 224 to Estacada, continue on Forest Road 46 past North Fork Reservoir to Indian Henry Campground, and in another 2 miles park at the Alder Flat lot on the right. The path winds 1 mile through old growth to a pure stand of white alders along the Clackamas.

For more, continue on Clackamas Road southeast another mile to Rainbow Campground and park on the right. Walk down Oak Creek Fork to the Clackamas River, then upstream 4 miles through old growth to Riverside Campground.

Northward, a similar riverfront trail with aged conifers follows the Salmon River near Mount Hood. From Highway 26 west of Zigzag, turn south on Salmon River Road and go 2.7 miles to the trailhead. Hike past big trees to the river, then upstream to a higher trailhead, and eventually to the Salmon-Huckleberry Wilderness.

Mount Hood, Mount Hood National Forest

OREGON

LOCATION
east of Portland

LENGTH
1 to 38 miles

DIFFICULTY
moderate to very strenuous

TREE SPECIES
subalpine firs, whitebark pines

HIGHLIGHTS
timberline forest, Mount Hood glaciers and snowfields

For an easily reached forest at timberline in the Cascade Mountains, park at Timberline Lodge on Mount Hood and step into alpine meadows with stands of subalpine firs, mountain hemlocks, and whitebark pines. Snow encrusts some of these weather-blown trees all winter. Climb or ski upward to krummholz, where the same species appear as wind-sculpted dwarfs, centuries old and beyond the reach of fire and most insect pests. Mount Hood shines in perfect summertime compositions of green forest, white snow, blue sky, and multi-colored meadows in bloom.

Any length of walk here is rewarding; from the lodge, head uphill on the paved path. Peel off where fancy takes you, or join the Pacific Crest Trail with its unlimited possibilities north and south. Or press upward to ridgelines with bleached whitebark pines reduced to starkly bare trunks. These may have died a century ago, but they still protect living trees in their lee from harsh winds at alpine heights—a beautiful illustration of continuity and the younger generation's dependence on trees that came earlier.

For the hardcore, a 38-mile extravaganza circumnavigates the mountain with 9,000 feet of gross climb and icy stream crossings likely too high for prudent fording until late summer, so August and September are best for this trek. Ancient forests alternate with views to clear-cuts dating to the 1980s on lower slopes. New, even-aged plantations there are a poor substitute for the old-growth majesty that once encircled this landmark mountain.

From Portland, take Highway 26 east to Sandy and Government Camp, turn left on Timberline Highway, and continue to the lodge.

Notorious for deep snow, Mount Hood and its mountain hemlocks above Timberline Lodge become a winter wonderland.

OPPOSITE: Subalpine and noble firs have perfected their means of either shedding or accommodating heavy snow loads on the flanks of Mount Hood.

Mount Rainier National Park

WASHINGTON

LOCATION
southeast of Tacoma

LENGTH
1 to 93 miles

DIFFICULTY
easy to very strenuous

TREE SPECIES
subalpine firs, whitebark
pines, Pacific silver firs,
Alaska yellow cedars

HIGHLIGHTS
timberline forest, glaciers,
meadows, summit views

At 14,410 feet, Mount Rainier is the queen of north-western peaks, only 95 feet shorter than Mount Whitney's rise in the southern Sierra Nevada. The rounded summit topping Washington's Cascade Mountains represents a deity to many and a climax in the region's lineup of stratovolcanoes, including Shasta, Hood, Adams, and Baker. Timberline forests, where snowdrifts linger all summer, are captivating in green-on-white. Robust groves contrast with the gray ash and pumice of volcanic eruptions, and one might argue for Rainier as the ultimate in bold mountain elegance. Both timberline and deep woods are accessible, with paved roads to the highcountry, maintained trails, and all the amenities of the national park. Stroll the interface of forest, meadow, and tree line just out the door of the

Paradise Inn. Snowfall here in 1972 totaled 94 feet—a world record then for measured depths.

Take any of the stunning trails past subalpine conifers to glacier edges. Or launch a landmark backpacking adventure in and out of multiple forest zones from dwarf subalpine firs to ancient Douglas firs along cascading rivers. For the full menu, fit hikers can backpack the Wonderland Trail's 93-mile circumnavigation with a whopping gross gain of 22,000 feet. Three ranger stations welcome food caches for circuit hikers. Inquire with the Park Service, see Tami Asars's *Hiking the Wonderland Trail*, and apply for a permit early, as numbers are wisely limited.

From I-5, take Highway 7 in the north or Highway 12 in the south and drive eastward toward Park Route 706 and up to the Paradise Inn.

On the lower slopes of Mount Rainier, a vine maple and western hemlock share their spot in the sun.

OPPOSITE: Subalpine firs darken timberline slopes of Mount Rainier at sunrise. With narrow spires and stiff, short branches, these trees minimize the snow load they must bear and thrive where others would perish under accumulations of 20 feet or more. The firs also regenerate through the "layering" of lower limbs, which sag to the ground, sprout their own roots, and grow into new seedlings with parental shelter above them.

Sauk and North Fork Sauk Rivers, Mount Baker-Snoqualmie National Forest

WASHINGTON

LOCATION
south of Darrington

LENGTH
1-mile out and back

DIFFICULTY
easy

TREE SPECIES
western redcedars, western hemlocks

HIGHLIGHTS
river-bottom forest in the North Cascades

In the extraordinary empire of the North Cascade Mountains, dozens of forest trails appeal. Two are included here for their big trees, scenic riverfronts, and ease of access in Mount Baker-Snoqualmie National Forest.

A low-key Sauk River woodland walk loops through an ancient forest of conifers brightened by bigleaf and vine maples along a wild river rushing from glaciers. From Darrington (northeast of Everett), drive south on Darrington-Clear Creek Road on the southwest side of the Sauk River for about 4 miles and look for a minor parking area on the left. Take the trail downriver, or upstream if you happen to end up at a lower trail access—either works. If you drive to the Sauk River Bridge and tributary White Chuck River, go back 2 miles.

Driving farther south on Darrington-Clear Creek Road, cross the Sauk and stay right on Mountain Loop Highway/Forest Road 20. In 6 miles, turn left on North Fork Sauk Road/Forest Route 49, and go 8 miles to the end at North Fork Sauk Trail—excellent through riverfront forest and into the otherworldly Glacier Peak Wilderness. Late summer is best at this rainy, snowy wonderland.

Western redcedars and western hemlocks—typical of an uncut forest in the rain belt at lower elevations of the North Cascade Mountains—preside along the Sauk River.

FOLLOWING SPREAD: A vine maple morphs to autumn's red and yellow at the Sauk River.

Hoh River, Olympic National Park

WASHINGTON

LOCATION
southwest of Port Angeles, south of Forks

LENGTH
1 to 36 miles out and back, or more

DIFFICULTY
easy to very strenuous

TREE SPECIES
Sitka spruces, western redcedars, western hemlocks, bigleaf maples

HIGHLIGHTS
temperate rain forest, glacial edge

The riverfront trails of western Olympic National Park fill a class by themselves as showcases of temperate rain forests, and the Hoh River Trail is the ultimate for both easy access and big trees. Like the sequoia and redwood walks of California, this is a prize for forest-trail aficionados, but far more remote from the mainstream of the West Coast.

Start at the visitor center on the Spruce Nature Trail. Walk east and up the Hoh any distance; memorable trees await from the beginning. Sitka spruces reach seven feet across, western redcedars grow even thicker, and western hemlocks reach maximum girth for their kind as well. A walk of 1 mile out and back reveals much, but the more you look, the more you see.

The Hoh River Trail is essentially flat for 13 miles and then for 5 miles tilts up 4,300 feet to the Glacier Meadows campsite at the trail's end.

As elevation rises, tree sizes diminish and species change, for example, from western to mountain hemlocks. But giants persist. When backpacking, take bear precautions. Food canisters are required for the Sol Duc basin to the north; they're a good idea here too. The full course is a 36-mile multiday out and back to the base of Blue Glacier on the north flank of Mount Olympus—accessible, at that point, to equipped and experienced glacier climbers.

At 7,965 feet, Olympus is the highest peak in the Coast Ranges between Canada and the Los Angeles basin. Along with Mounts Rainier and Baker in Washington's Cascade Mountains, this is also the most glacier-covered mountain south of British Columbia, with immense layers of ice, gaping crevasses and bergschrunds, and a jumbled chaos of seracs in all stages of tumbling descent as the glaciers migrate downslope to terminal moraines.

A shelf fungus thrives along the Hoh River Trail.

OPPOSITE: The Hoh River Trail makes for a classic tour of the Pacific Northwest's temperate rain forest. Here, on a rainy day, the hemlocks, Sitka spruces, western redcedars, and grand firs rise high in saturated air.

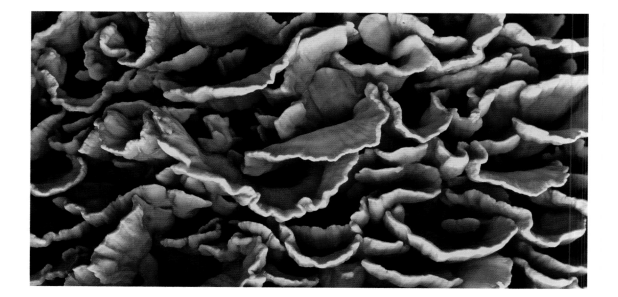

For a sunny break from the rain forest, hikers can wander out to the gravel bars and shorelines of the Hoh River as it riffles from the Mount Olympus highlands.

OPPOSITE: This view from the High Hoh Bridge over the upper Hoh River looks down to western redcedars and mountain hemlocks north of Mount Olympus.

The Hoh route also connects to the larger trail network in Olympic National Park and companion hikes through some of the continent's most remarkable conifer forests.

Downstream from the national park boundary, the Hoh River basin was fully owned by the timber industry, but in the 1990s the Western Rivers Conservancy launched a program to acquire 90 percent of the riverfront for protection, sponsoring one of the premier river and forest restoration efforts nationwide.

This is also one of the rainiest locations in the United States, with drenching amounts not even measured in the backcountry. Olympus's heights get some of the deepest snow anywhere. Expect precipitation at any time, but the best bet for clear skies is May or June, when a sunny day in a rain forest is truly splendid. The weather might clear for windows to blue sky from April through September, but it might not, even if you stay awhile, so take an umbrella and waterproof gear. Expect relentless rainfall in autumn. Precipitation at the trailhead often comes as rain even in the dead of winter, with heavy snow higher up.

Take Highway 101 (west side of the Olympic Peninsula loop) to the Hoh River turnoff south of Forks and drive up the valley to the visitor center.

Quinault River, Olympic National Park

LOCATION
western Olympic Peninsula

LENGTH
36 miles out and back, with shorter or longer hikes

DIFFICULTY
easy to moderate

TREE SPECIES
Sitka spruces, western redcedars, western hemlocks, bigleaf maples

HIGHLIGHTS
one of the finest temperate rain forests

Bigleaf maples—decked out with mosses, lichens, and sword ferns—have turned yellow in October at a sunlit opening along the Quinault River. Largest of the maple family, and rivaling some of the largest deciduous trees nationwide, bigleaf maples grow to six-foot diameters and 125-foot heights, producing seeds that are a favorite of squirrels.

Much like the Hoh River northward, only less visited, the Quinault River flows from heights of the Olympic Mountains to the Pacific Ocean by crossing one of the most extraordinary ancient temperate forests worldwide. The Valley of the Giants harbors six champion trees—the largest of their species. Only California's sequoia and coast redwood groves have larger trees.

A western redcedar, 20 feet in diameter, stands off North Shore Road along a path across from Lake Quinault Resort—reportedly the largest tree in the world outside California. The largest yellow cedar, 38 feet in diameter, is up the Quinault Trail. The largest Douglas fir, 13 feet thick, hides remotely in the Quinault Research Natural Area. The largest Sitka spruce, 1,000 years old and 18 feet in diameter, is off South Shore Road near the Rain Forest Resort Village Trail. The largest western hemlock, nine feet in diameter, is in Enchanted Valley, and a mountain hemlock six feet in diameter grows nearby. Seeking out most of these giants is extremely difficult and not necessary, as the entire trail reveals ancient forest all along the way, and a hemlock that's five feet in diameter is just about as impressive as one that's six feet.

Hike up the well-trod path through grove after grove. At 13 miles, the trail enters Enchanted Valley, where encircling peaks earn the name. Backpackers can continue for a trans-Olympic expedition, topping Anderson Pass and then descending the Dosewallips River to road access on the east side of the park, though the highway shuttle for this crossing seems endless. I prefer to hike out and back and maximize trail time without the extra drive.

For the lower Quinault trailhead, go to Aberdeen and drive Highway 101 north along the

coast 44 miles. Turn east just before Lake Quinault, ascend South Shore Road 19 miles with care to stay right at the North Fork Road bridge, and continue to the trailhead at the end.

The nearby Queets River likewise tempts with an old-growth trail, but that hike begins with one of the longest fords I've ever waded, dangerous or impossible at times, and with the possibility of getting stuck on the other side; watch the forecast! The Bogachiel and Sol Duc Rivers also have fine forest trails on the west side of the Olympic Mountains. Forest lovers who don't mind dampness could spend a month here.

OPPOSITE: A fallen western redcedar's root mass endures for ages along the floodplain of the Quinault River.

At a tributary to the Quinault River, vine maples cling to their autumn leaves while the larger bigleaf maples' foliage has fallen. Mountain hemlocks and alders darken the background.

Duckabush and Hamma Hamma Rivers, Olympic National Park

WASHINGTON

LOCATION
northwest of Olympia

LENGTH
1 to 8 miles out and back

DIFFICULTY
strenuous

TREE SPECIES
western hemlocks, western redcedars, bigleaf maples

HIGHLIGHTS
old-growth rain forest

The Hamma Hamma woodland trail follows the river's cascading descent from Olympic Mountain heights with vine maple leaves like constellations of stars along the shore.

FOLLOWING SPREAD: In the Olympic rain forest, moss blankets this boulder along the Hamma Hamma canyon trail (left). Padded in moss, a bigleaf maple clings to its autumn leaves along the Duckabush River Trail. Still green, a cascara tree rises on the left (top right). Through Olympic National Forest, the Duckabush River Trail climbs toward the Olympic National Park boundary. Douglas firs, western hemlocks, and western redcedars thrive here in The Brothers Wilderness (bottom right).

Virtually any trail up any valley in Olympic National Park is a tree lovers' hiking treat of a lifetime, and the lesser-known Duckabush and Hamma Hamma River valleys on the southeast quadrant of the peninsula are no exception.

For miles these trails penetrate dripping forests of hoary conifers. The Duckabush ascends the length of its canyon, with options of backtracking or climbing out north to the Dosewallips or Quinault River basins or south to the Skokomish River. The Hamma Hamma climbs through a similar rainforest canyon and veers upward to the trail's end at Mildred Lakes.

From Olympia, drive north on the eastern arm of Highway 101 (Olympic Loop Highway, east side) past Shelton and beyond to the wide spot of Eldon. Turn west on Hamma Hamma River Road/Forest Road 25, and continue to the trailhead. For the Duckabush River's longer trail, drive north on Highway 101 for 9 more miles to Duckabush Road, turn west, and go to the end.

Admiralty Island, Tongass National Forest

ALASKA

LOCATION
south of Juneau

LENGTH
2 miles off-trail

DIFFICULTY
strenuous

TREE SPECIES
Sitka spruces, western hemlocks, Alaska yellow cedars

HIGHLIGHTS
uncut rain forest of Southeast Alaska

Admiralty Island rises above Snug Cove in Gambier Bay, where backcountry routes—but no trails—climb to an overlook of Alaska's southeastern rainforest wilderness.

Tongass is the largest of all the national forests, covering 16.7 million acres including much of Alaska's southern panhandle and stretching a mind-boggling 500 miles from British Columbia northward to Glacier Bay National Park and Preserve. It's like going from Mexico to San Francisco and having it *all* be forest in various degrees of protection or not—including 1,000 islands, 11,000 miles of shoreline, and one-third of the planet's remaining temperate old growth, along with salmon in numbers like those that once filled rivers of the Pacific Northwest (though the fish here are also troubled).

Large areas of Tongass were clear-cut under a federal law that for decades gave $40 million per year in federal taxpayer subsidies to timber companies. Even more comprehensively, native economic development corporations clear-cut most of their 540,000 acres. A fiefdom of Alaska's congressional delegation, the Forest Service in the 1960s planned to mow 95 percent of the Tongass—which is to say much of the virgin temperate rain forest left on earth.

However, hard-earned legislation in 1980 set aside 14 wilderness areas of 5.8 million acres. The big trees are mostly limited to valley bottoms and low-elevation slopes because rock, ice, and snow dominate not far above sea level. Beyond that sensible restraint, most of the unprotected old growth remaining was set aside by an insightful roadless designation in 2001 under Forest Service Chief Mike Dombeck. However, the Trump Administration attempted to open 9.2 million acres of roadless Tongass terrain for logging in 2020—even though, according to federal data, cutting there the year before resulted in a net loss of $17.7 million for the Forest Service, and even though 96 percent of the

16,000 letters of public comment supported keeping the logging restrictions in place. Challenges to the roadless rule are unresolved as of this writing.

Admiralty Island remains one of the Tongass crown jewels: 937,000 acres of ancient forests, mountains, fjords, and salmon streams. Near-total logging had been planned, but the island was made a national monument in 1978, and two years later, under the Alaska National Interest Lands Conservation Act, much of it was designated wilderness in one of the Tongass's largest reserves. The Forest Service maintains 20 miles of trail—mostly boggy portage paths in the Cross Admiralty Canoe Route.

Though local paths lead out from many of Southeast Alaska's towns, few trails are well known for hiking in the Tongass, and travel is vexed by persistent rain totaling 200 inches in many areas. Mosquitoes, flies, and no-see-ums can be maddening, and the islands and mainland are populated by the greatest density of brown (grizzly) bears on earth, not to mention a ubiquitous shrub descriptively called devil's club. Seeing this wilderness is a bit of a challenge and, practically speaking, going anywhere in Tongass National Forest is beyond most people's reach and comfort level. But a book about forest walks in America is hardly complete without recognition of this place.

I was fortunate to boat to Admiralty Island with my friend and outfitter Andy Romanoff of Juneau, and he knew where we could beach and walk, so at Gambier Bay we hiked cross-country to overlooks of the wild forest below. Similar commercial guide services are available.

With access via the Alaska ferry system, short walks into the Tongass can more easily be taken

from Juneau at the Rainforest Trail on the north end of Douglas Island, from Ketchikan to Ward Lake, and at other towns reached by ferryboat. Sea kayaking is another viable way for competent paddlers to tour these forested shorelines, though foot travel once ashore is extremely limited.

TROPICAL ISLANDS

America's tropical islands lie on either side of the continent. Puerto Rico awaits 1,000 miles offshore from Florida, and Hawaii rises as a chain of volcanoes 2,500 miles across the Pacific—farther from the continents than any other land on earth.

Forests on these islands evolved in isolation for a time. But with the advent of sea travel and trade, the introduction of exotic plants and animals from elsewhere has taken an egregious toll on native trees and other life on both our island Edens.

In Hawaii—ground zero for exotic species invasions nationwide—virtually all land is affected by the onslaught. Even the picturesque coconut palms didn't evolve here, but their presence harks back centuries to the arrival of Polynesians in canoes. The only palm native to Hawaii is the loulu, a small fan-palm family of 16 species, imperiled because exotic rats eat the seeds. Plus, whole forests of loulu were cleared for farming and settlement. Most native tree species were likewise decimated by the forces of development.

Still, some native forests survive, and the junglelike thickets of trees, shrubs, vines, and ground cover make a fascinating tropical counterpart to our mainland forests. State parks, county parks, and Hawai'i Volcanoes National Park all offer trails through these Pacific islands.

In Puerto Rico, public land is limited, but in 1876 King Alfonso XII of Spain designated El Yunque as a preserve. In 1898, after Spain was forced to cede Puerto Rico to the United States, President Theodore Roosevelt had the good sense to name El Yunque a forest reserve of our own. At 29,000 acres, this is now one of our smallest national forests. Ecosystems of this special area would benefit by expansion of the protected area to headwater reaches.

Winter is the time to visit and explore these reserves with their tantalizing escapes from the chill of America's mainland. Puerto Rico is very hot and humid in summer. Hiking in Hawaii appeals year-round, with a temperate summer that's drier than the rest of the year and with calmer seas. Yet, given the weather elsewhere, winter is when most people want to escape to these Pacific islands.

El Yunque National Forest

PUERTO RICO

LOCATION
northeast end of the island

LENGTH
2 miles or more out and back

DIFFICULTY
moderate to strenuous

TREE SPECIES
ausubo, palo colorado, sierra palm

HIGHLIGHTS
eastern tropical forest

El Yunque National Forest harbors 225 native tree species and not a single one of them grows wild on the American mainland. So, for anyone who wants to increase their life list of tree species seen, this is the place! Some trees are 1,000 years old. Twenty-three plants are known as endemic here—found nowhere else on earth—and many more are simply not yet documented.

Annual rainfall at mountain heights totals a drippy 200 inches, and torrential cloudbursts can drench hikers at any time with up to two-and-a-half inches in a single hour. May to November is wettest, and summer is hot, so I made my pilgrimage when tropical weather was delightful—in April. As do others; the busy tourist season runs from January to May. The national forest does not allow camping, and few opportunities lie outside, so make arrangements at hotels or bed-and-breakfasts nearby. Limited primitive camping may open by permit as the Forest Service recovers from the hurricanes of 2017—a work in progress even several years later.

Miles of trail can be walked to tropical canyons, waterfalls, and mountaintops covered with sierra palms, whose fruits are a favorite of endangered Puerto Rican parrots, which also need large trees for nesting cavities. The flashy green-and-red birds—which may have numbered one million at European contact in the 16th century—were sadly reduced to only 13 individuals in 1975 in an extinction crisis comparable to that of the better-known whooping crane on the American mainland. Recovery efforts suffered setbacks with Hurricane Maria in 2017, but fortunately the biologists' strategy of establishing a backup population on the other side of the island at Río Abajo State Forest and a captive breeding program provided a safety net against extinction.

The Big Tree Trail is a 2-mile out and back through forest including a monumental ausubo tree. The La Coca Trail descends through vine-clad rain forest to the wild Río Mameyes, 7 miles out and back. El Yunque Peak Trail, 6 miles both ways, climbs to the summit, thick with sierra palms but still offering views to startlingly blue waters of the Atlantic Ocean.

Catch a flight from East Coast cities to San Juan, rent a car, and drive to El Yunque at the eastern end of the island. For trails, get timely tips at the visitor center along the forest entrance road.

PREVIOUS SPREAD: Sierra palms cover mountains of El Yunque National Forest in Puerto Rico.

An emerald anole lizard appears along the La Coca Trail at the Río de la Mina.

OPPOSITE: In the United States' finest eastern tropical rain forest, the Río de la Mina plunges over a waterfall along the Big Tree Trail of El Yunque National Forest.

Kīlauea Iki Trail, Hawai'i Volcanoes National Park

HAWAII

LOCATION
east of Kīlauea Visitor Center, Big Island

LENGTH
5 miles out and back or less

DIFFICULTY
moderate

TREE SPECIES
hāpu'u (Hawaiian tree fern), 'ōhi'a

HIGHLIGHTS
tree ferns, junglelike understory next to an active volcano

A tree fern, or hāpu'u, unfurls its fronds on the rainforest trail near the Kīlauea Crater in Hawai'i Volcanoes National Park.

Near Hawai'i Volcanoes National Park's visitor center, this rainforest trail offers a striking contrast to the adjacent landscape of the world's most active volcano. Downslope and outside the crater's rim, the path leads to a moist tropical wonderland of dense vegetation and dramatic lava features. The trail was closed by eruptions in 2018, reopened in 2019, and closed again in 2020; check with the Park Service for current status.

Tree ferns reach 40 feet. Once plentiful and thriving on the windward (east) sides of the Hawaiian Islands between 1,000 and 6,000 feet, the giant ferns are now harder to find, but this grove persists within the park.

On another section of trail, 'ōhi'a trees take many forms, from prostrate pioneers on recently hardened lava to crowns 80 feet high in damp soil. This broadleaf evergreen with showy red-to-yellow flowers is the most common native tree on the islands, and it is revered by native Hawaiians. However, an exotic fungus has killed many trees on the Big Island—as well as Kauai, O'ahu, and Maui—since discovery of the pathogen in 2014. The fungus is spread in soil, so clean your shoes after hiking. Park rangers recommend hosing tires after driving on dirt roads. Some trees appear to be resistant, so there is hope that they will survive and recolonize.

From the park visitor center, go south on Chain of Craters Road 2 miles to the Kīlauea Iki parking lot. Take the Crater Rim Trail to the left and onto the Kīlauea Iki Trail, which passes through the rain forest. Beyond, the trail (if open) drops 400 feet to the Kīlauea caldera.

From Hilo, drive south on Highway 11 past the community of Volcano, turn left into the visitor center, and check with rangers for trail conditions.

Puʻuhonua o Hōnaunau National Historical Park

HAWAII

Coconut palms are not native to Hawaii, meaning they were not there before people arrived. But they came with Polynesian mariners who canoed halfway across the Pacific beginning 1,000 years ago, and the iconic fruitful trees seem at home and have become a beloved and "naturalized" symbol of the islands.

Palms can be seen in many areas, but a magnificent grove waves in Pacific breezes at the Puʻuhonua o Hōnaunau National Historical Park of 180 acres, chiefly known for its cultural and historic values. Thickets of green broadleaf naupaka shrubbery grow under the trees. Stroll there and walk on shoreline rocks with views back to the tall, curved trunks waving in the breeze above white coral sand and black lava bedrock at tide line.

From Kailua-Kona, take Highway 11 to Captain Cook and on to Keokea. Turn west on Highway 160 and continue to the national historical park.

Coconut palms flex in the afternoon breeze above the blackened lava shores at Puʻuhonua o Hōnaunau National Historical Park.

OPPOSITE: Coconut palms shade the shoreline at this park while three-foot-high naupaka shrubs fill the understory.

Alaka'i Swamp, Kōke'e State Park

HAWAII

This forest of the Alaka'i Wilderness Preserve grows on the slopes of Mount Wai'ale'ale, rising 5,148 feet and averaging 450 inches of rain a year—the third-highest precipitation regularly monitored in the world (the top two sites are in India). At the end of Highway 550, the Kōke'e Lodge and Museum has maps and current trail assessments.

Steep, muddy, slippery, predictably wet and rainy, and surprisingly cool for Hawaii, this hike penetrates rainforest vegetation like most of us will never see. A confusing network of trails has accumulated from past eras of management, but the main route, partly on boardwalks, aims upward through the swamp.

Trees are small but densely packed and entirely different from anything on the American mainland. 'Ōlapa have whimsically hand-shaped leaves. Tree ferns grow tall with their harkening to an entirely different epoch; the Mesozoic and its giant reptiles may come to mind. Some areas of the mountain are relatively barren owing to a timberline of wetness—there's too much water for trees to grow. For hikers who persist to the top, and arrive at a rare clear moment, the lookout, Kilohana, opens to views across the upland crest of Kauai to the Pacific far below.

From the southwest side of the island, drive to Waimea, turn north on Highway 550, and climb past the Waimea Canyon overlook—but not without pausing to admire this Grand Canyon of the islands. Proceed to the end of Highway 550, then continue on the road to Pu'u o Kila and the trailhead. Here, at the westernmost outpost, our tour of America's forest trails comes to an end.

LOCATION
north of Waimea, Kauai

LENGTH
7 miles out and back or less

DIFFICULTY
wet, slippery

TREE SPECIES
'ōlapa, 'ōhi'a, tree ferns

HIGHLIGHTS
third-wettest place on earth, world's highest rainforest swamp

In the heart of the Alaka'i Swamp, dense vegetation thrives at the wettest place in the Western Hemisphere.

BEYOND A WALK IN THE WOODS

Woodland trails take us to serenity and satisfaction, to discoveries in exciting places, and perhaps to rediscoveries in forests where we know every step but can always find something new.

We need our forests, and we love them, which is a powerful combination. So it's only natural that—for many of us—walking on woodland trails is considered a part of living well, and what we see when we're among the trees can lead to even greater meaning beyond the satisfaction of simply recognizing beauty all around us.

The trails featured in this book take us to places that are natural. Walking these trails is good for us through every year of our lives, through every season as the forests cycle in their rhythms of the ages, and through every day that we step into the real world that awaits.

Woodlands are threatened now as never before because of a collision of values and the resulting firestorm of harm. These threats include industrial logging that unnecessarily ravages rather than sustains the life and productivity of forests, unlimited growth with development that sacrifices all that's wild, and the climate crisis that throws doubt on the entire fate of the earth. Global warming inevitably forces a cascade of damage from droughts, floods, fires, and invasions of exotic species that disrupt intricate balances and delicate workings of a world that has evolved for millennia to produce the fruitfulness we've known.

I leave it to other media and messengers to document the details and consequences of those threats and, instead, I make the case for simply caring about the fate of our forests. A walk in the woods is—at once—the most superficial and most profound act one might take toward a new regard for the earth and toward the changes needed to reverse trajectories of loss. Here is where we might find the reason, the motivation, and the determination to care not just for the woods but for all the planet in the stormy days of physical, cultural, and political upheaval that press upon us.

Something more than a walk in the woods might occur on the path ahead. Take that first step out the door and into the forest around you, and see where it leads you to go.

Early morning fog begins to clear in the redwood forest of California's Del Norte Coast Redwoods State Park.

SUGGESTED READING

For more trails, hiking guides to virtually all our states and major parks are available; search online, at your local bookstore, or in park visitor centers. Guidebooks specifically for old-growth trees are by Bates, Kershner and Leverett, LeGue, and Van Pelt. If you've enjoyed this book, consider my earlier woodland works, *Trees and Forests of America* and *Twilight of the Hemlocks and Beeches*. The following is a short list of what I've found compelling, informative, and beautiful.

Arno, Stephen F. and Ramona P. Hammerly, *Timberline: Mountain and Arctic Forest Frontiers*.

Bates, John, *Our Living Ancestors: The History and Ecology of Old-Growth Forests in Wisconsin and Where to Find Them*.

Berger, John J., *Understanding Forests*.

Davis, Mary Byrd, ed., *Eastern Old-Growth Forests: Prospects for Rediscovery and Recovery*.

Devall, Bill, ed., *Clearcut: The Tragedy of Industrial Forestry*.

Durbin, Kathie, *Tree Huggers: Victory, Defeat, and Renewal in the Northwest Ancient Forest Campaign*.

Ferguson, Gary, *Land on Fire: The New Reality of Wildfire in the West*.

Finch, Bill, Beth Maynor Young, Rhett Johnson, and John C. Hall, *Longleaf, Far as the Eye Can See: A New Vision of North America's Richest Forest*.

Foster, David R., ed., *Hemlock: A Forest Giant on the Edge*.

Haskell, David George, *The Forest Unseen: A Year's Watch in Nature*.

Hays, Samuel P., *Wars in the Woods: The Rise of Ecological Forestry in America*.

Heinrich, Bernd, *The Trees in My Forest*.

Kauffmann, Michael, *Conifer Country: A Natural History and Hiking Guide to 35 Conifers of the Klamath Mountain Region*.

Keator, Glenn, *The Life of an Oak: An Intimate Portrait*.

Kershner, Bruce and Robert T. Leverett, *The Sierra Club Guide to the Ancient Forests of the Northeast*.

Kirk, Ruth and Charles Mauzy, eds., *The Enduring Forests: Northern California, Oregon, Washington, British Columbia, and Southeast Alaska*.

Kodas, Michael, *Megafire: The Race to Extinguish a Deadly Epidemic of Flame*.

Kricher, John and Gordon Morrison, *California and Pacific Northwest Forests*.

Lansky, Mitch, *Beyond the Beauty Strip: Saving What's Left of Our Forests*.

LeGue, Chandra, *Oregon's Ancient Forests: A Hiking Guide*.

Little, Charles E., *The Dying of the Trees: The Pandemic in America's Forests*.

Maloof, Joan, *Nature's Temples: The Complex World of Old-Growth Forests*.

Norse, Elliott A., *Ancient Forests of the Pacific Northwest*.

Peattie, Donald Culross, *A Natural History of Western Trees* and *A Natural History of Trees of Eastern and Central North America*.

Petrides, George A. and Janet Wehr, *Eastern Trees*.

Petrides, George A. and Olivia Petrides, *Western Trees*.

Sutton, Ann and Myron Sutton, *Eastern Forests*.

Suzuki, David and Wayne Grady, *Tree: A Life Story*.

Van Pelt, Robert, *Forest Giants of the Pacific Coast*.

Wohlleben, Peter, *The Hidden Life of Trees: What They Feel, How They Communicate*.

Vine maples complement the reflected green of Oregon's McKenzie River in its dark forest of conifers.

ABOUT THE PHOTOGRAPHS

For many years I used a Canon A-1 camera with 17-200mm FD lenses, but most of the photos here were taken with a Canon 5D digital camera with 17-200mm L-series zoom lenses and a 50mm L-series lens. For adventures when a small kit was needed, I carried a Fujifilm digital X-E2 with its 18-55mm and 55-200mm XF zoom lenses.

With the goal of showing landscapes as accurately and realistically as possible, I limit myself to minor postphoto adjustments for aperture, contrast, and color under Apple's most basic photo program. I use no artificial light or filters, and do nothing to alter the content of the photos. The overriding principle of my work is to share with others the beauty and adventures that I've been privileged to see and experience in the natural world.

Tulip trees, red oaks, sugar maples, and basswoods create a canopy that lights up at dawn in Rock Creek Park of Washington, DC.

ACKNOWLEDGMENTS

My wife, Ann Vileisis, has provided a constant reminder that nature is beautiful, that our time here is precious, and that our loving care of the earth and of each other is essential. Her ideas, inspiration, encouragement, photo modeling, logistical support, and hiking companionship have made my walks in the woods and my greater journey through life not just possible but exquisite in both routine and exceptional ways. I will forever appreciate her time away from her own writing career and from her inspired work to protect the environment where we live on the coast of southern Oregon.

Associate publisher Jim Muschett at Rizzoli supported this and previous books in what has incrementally become a series. This volume, plus *America's Great River Journeys* and *America's Great Mountain Trails*, now form a trilogy about experiencing nature in America and exploring our greater home outdoors. It was a pleasure working with Jim and his team: the extremely capable production manager and editor Candice Fehrman, the brilliant designer Susi Oberhelman, and the dedicated publicist Jessica Napp.

The endpaper map was produced by Cartagram's Steven Gordon—not only a fine cartographer but also an artist who was eager to create exactly what was needed.

For logistical help including rides to trailheads, pickups late in the day, overnight lodging, tips about where to go, review of manuscript sections, and information by phone, email, and interview, thanks to: Greg and Mary Bettencourt, Cayucos, California; Tinelle Bustam, U.S. Forest Service, Puerto Rico and Washington, DC; Denny Caneff, Wisconsin; Ken Cline, College of the Atlantic, Bar Harbor, Maine; Rebecca Cole-Will, Acadia National Park; Don Elder, Bend, Oregon; Rolf Gubler, Shenandoah National Park; Ben Hayes, Hawai'i Volcanoes National Park; Gabe Howe, Siskiyou Mountain Club, Ashland, Oregon; Kristine Johnson, Great Smoky Mountains National Park; Carolyn Krupp, El Yunque National Forest; Chandra LeGue, author of *Oregon's Ancient Forests*; Robert Leverett, master of old-growth measurement, Florence, Massachusetts; Dale Luthringer, Cook Forest State Park; Jim Palmer, brother, hiking companion, and member of Friends of Patapsco Valley State Park, Maryland; Justin Petty, Idaho Nature Conservancy; Holly Richter, Arizona Water Projects Director, The Nature Conservancy; Andy Romanoff, adventure guide, Juneau, Alaska; Becky Schmitz, sister and lover of hemlocks and dogwoods, Charlottesville, Virginia; Stephen P. Schmitz, nephew and Virginia mountains guide; Nick Shema, Volcano, Hawai'i; and Allyson Siwik and Donna Stevens, Gila River stewards, New Mexico.

The superb work of Bruce Kershner and Robert Leverett in *The Sierra Club Guide to the Ancient Forests of the Northeast* was especially helpful in locating and understanding old-growth forests of that region. Likewise, Robert Van Pelt's *Forest Giants of the Pacific Coast* is a landmark work of science and art. See more under Suggested Reading.

Douglas irises bloom at the forest's edge in Oregon's Port Orford Heads State Park. Thousands of these flowers make early May the prime time to visit here.

First published in the United States of America in 2021 by
Rizzoli International Publications, Inc.
300 Park Avenue South
New York, NY 10010
www.rizzoliusa.com

Publisher: Charles Miers
Associate Publisher: James Muschett
Managing Editor: Lynn Scrabis
Editor: Candice Fehrman
Design: Susi Oberhelman
Text and Photographs: Tim Palmer
Endpaper Map: Steven Gordon, Cartagram

Printed in China

2021 2022 2023 2024 / 10 9 8 7 6 5 4 3 2 1

ISBN: 978-0-8478-6757-8

Library of Congress Control Number: 2021934377

Visit us online:
Facebook.com/RizzoliNewYork
Twitter: @Rizzoli_Books
Instagram.com/RizzoliBooks
Pinterest.com/RizzoliBooks
Youtube.com/user/RizzoliNY
Issuu.com/Rizzoli

CAPTIONS FOR PHOTOS ON THE OPENING PAGES OF THIS BOOK:

PAGE 1: Carson Hicks explores the wonders of Jedediah Smith Redwoods State Park in California.
PAGES 2–3: Western redcedar trees stand tall at the Bernard DeVoto Grove in Idaho's Nez Perce-Clearwater National Forest.
PAGES 4–5: Sugar maple, red maple, and striped maple leaves color the ground at Heart Lake in the Adirondack Mountains of New York.
PAGES 6–7: A valley oak darkens to silhouette in sunset light at Eastman Lake in California.

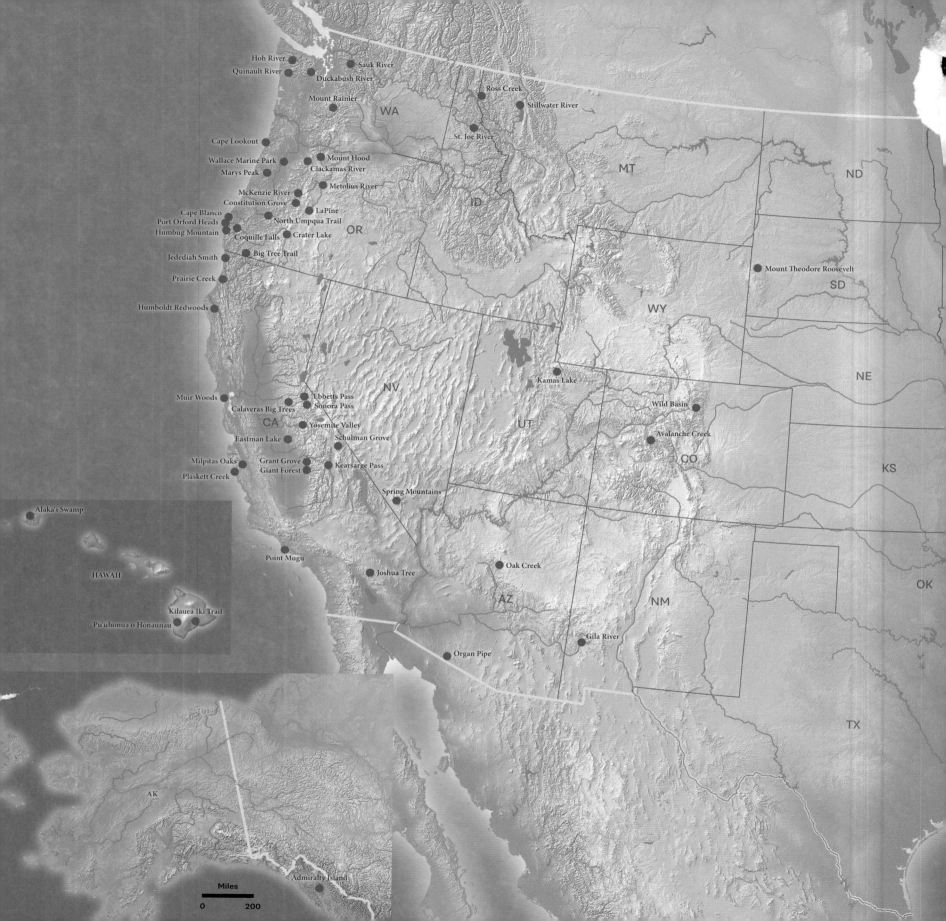

Hoh River
Quinault River
Sauk River
Duckabush River

Mount Rainier
WA

Cape Lookout

Wallace Marine Park
Marys Peak

Mount Hood
Clackamas River

McKenzie River
Constitution Grove
Cape Blanco
Port Orford Heads
Humbug Mountain
Coquille Falls

Metolius River

LaPine
North Umpqua Trail
Crater Lake

Jedediah Smith
Big Tree Trail

Prairie Creek

Humboldt Redwoods

Ross Creek
Stillwater River

St. Joe River

MT

ND

ID

OR

Mount Theodore Roosevelt

SD

WY

Kamas Lake

Muir Woods

Calaveras Big Trees
CA

Eastman Lake

Milpitas Oaks
Plaskett Creek

Ebbetts Pass
Sonora Pass

Yosemite Valley

Schulman Grove

Grant Grove
Giant Forest

Kearsarge Pass

NV

UT

Wild Basin

Avalanche Creek

CO

NE

KS

Spring Mountains

Alaka'i Swamp

HAWAII

Point Mugu

Joshua Tree

Oak Creek

OK

Kilauea Iki Trail
Pu'uhonua o Hōnaunau

AZ

NM

Gila River

Organ Pipe

TX

AK

Admiralty Island

Miles

0   200